BASIC BOOKS IN EDUCATION

Editor: *Kathleen O'Connor, B.Sc., Senior
Lecturer in Education, Rolle College, Exmouth*
Advisory Editor: *D. J. O'Connor, M.A., Ph.D., Professor of
Philosophy, University of Exeter*

LEARNING

An Introduction
for Students of Education

This book *introduces* the student to the psychological
study of learning. It is intended as a starting-point.
It is hoped that ideas gained at a first reading will
inform tutorial discussion, provide background for
lectures and further study and, most importantly, lead
to fuller understanding of observations and experiences as well as to readier evaluation of educational
problems and innovations.

Key words in the text are in SMALL CAPITALS,
there are summaries and 'further reading' lists at the
end of each chapter and there is a full bibliography,
glossary and index.

LEARNING

An Introduction
for Students of Education

KATHLEEN O'CONNOR, B.Sc.

SENIOR LECTURER IN EDUCATION
ROLLE COLLEGE, EXMOUTH

MACMILLAN
London · Melbourne · Toronto
1 9 6 8

Published by
MACMILLAN AND CO LTD
Little Essex Street London W C 2
and also at Bombay Calcutta and Madras
Macmillan South Africa (Publishers) Pty Ltd Johannesburg
The Macmillan Company of Australia Pty Ltd Melbourne
The Macmillan Company of Canada Ltd Toronto

Printed in Great Britain by
ROBERT MACLEHOSE AND CO LTD
The University Press, Glasgow

Contents

Preface

This book has been written primarily for students in Colleges of Education, and in the title the word *Introduction* should be taken literally. The book is intended, not to take the place of the many books on learning available for reference, but rather to provide a starting point. It is hoped that ideas gained at a first reading will inform tutorial discussion, provide background for lectures and further study and, most importantly, lead to fuller understanding of observations and experiences, as well as to readier evaluation of educational problems and innovations.

I am grateful to Mrs Isabel Pearson, who, as a student, read the manuscript and suggested some alterations leading to greater clarity.

KATHLEEN O'CONNOR

Acknowledgements

The author and publishers would like to thank the following, who have kindly given permission for the use of copyright material: Harcourt, Brace & World Inc. for the figures from *Introduction to Psychology,* by E. R. Hilgard; Methuen & Co. Ltd for extracts from *Cumulative Record,* by B. F. Skinner; and Routledge & Kegan Paul Ltd for the extract from *Behaviourism,* by J. B. Watson.

1 Introduction

Almost everything which we do when we are awake has been learned. We have learned to move in a host of different ways and to talk and write, perhaps in more than one language. We have learned to like this, dislike that, admire X, approve of Y, fear P and laugh at Q. We have learned the social customs of our society and perhaps to co-operate with group A and compete with group B. We have learned to play this instrument and to fashion that article. We can read. We know something of the language of mathematics and how to read maps, charts and other symbolic material. We have learned much about all that surrounds us in the world and how to set about solving certain kinds of problem. We have gained understanding of a number of subjects as well as of rules and theories applied in realms as different as games and physics, morals and politics. Perhaps, in some measure, we have learned to know ourselves.

An examination of this list will show that we learn vastly more than the knowledge and skills traditionally associated with educational psychology and academic work. Twentieth-century psychology has drawn attention to the importance of learned HABITS (and ATTITUDES) in the development of personality and of all forms of social behaviour. In consequence not only teachers but also psychotherapists and social workers are now very interested in learning processes. It is small wonder that psychologists frequently regard *learning* as the central process in understanding human behaviour.

THE STUDY OF LEARNING

A study of learning is part of the larger study of psychology, which may be defined as the scientific study of human experience and human and animal behaviour.

Psychology is both a biological science and a social science. It is *biological* in that it rests on the findings of biology – the structure and workings of the body, and in particular the nerves, brain and sense organs: and on genetics, the study of heredity and the influence of the environment on hereditary make-up. It is social in that the experience and development of human beings is continually affected by the social environment in which they live. Thus it is that there is a close connection between the study of psychology and the practice of social and industrial administration, law and criminology, politics, education and medicine. Psychological topics relevant to the practical tasks of education are growth and development, learning and thinking, individuality and personality; and knowledge of these can inform joint investigations of educational problems by educational psychologists, research workers, teachers and administrators.

Some students, readily accepting the position of psychology in relation to other sciences and to practical affairs, are surprised that it includes the study of animal behaviour. Psychologists, especially genetic or developmental psychologists, are interested in the origin and development of behaviour and experience in: (1) organisms ranging from the simplest to the most complex (i.e. man); and (2) individuals from birth, through maturity, to old age. It is accepted that when attempting to understand the behaviour of a child we frequently look to his past experience for possible explanations. But students are sometimes surprised that psychologists look to the behaviour of other animals to gain understanding of the behaviour and experience of *homo sapiens*. The tradition stems from the evolutionary biology which followed the publication in 1859 of Darwin's *Origin of Species*. Anatomical continuity between various species suggested also continuity in behaviour and in psychological processes such as learning. By observing learning in various species, knowledge has been gained of some basic processes fundamental to learning wherever it occurs. Though the same, or very similar, processes may be found operating in relation to the learning of, say, cats, pigeons, rats, monkeys, apes and men, yet it is always necessary to look at the total learning situation and observe important differences as well as resemblances, between learning in varied species. With this proviso ever in mind, the student should be able to appreciate the relevance of comparative animal studies in psychology.

There is, however, another reason for the use of animals by psychologists and this will be better understood after a consideration of what is meant by *scientific* study. The findings of scientific study rely on a careful assessment of *evidence* obtained by observation, experiment and measurement. Observation gives knowledge of fact in the only way that it can be obtained at first hand. Experiment is observation under conditions which are planned and controlled. Measurement permits expression of findings in as exact a manner as possible and in a way that can be publicly checked. Such experiment in psychology, the study of behaviour, must of necessity involve restriction of the SUBJECTS of the experiments. Frequently to put these necessary restrictions upon human beings is either impracticable or banned by ethical considerations. In consequence, animals are often used as subjects for psychological experiments. Although findings from such experiments must be used with caution, they can often point the way to subsequent study of human beings in less restricted and more complex situations.

The control of subjects and the assessment of experimental evidence common to all scientific investigations is, of course, necessary when investigating the problems of education. An example from educational research will serve to illustrate the method. Imagine an infant school where, after exactly two years of schooling, each child is given a reading test, and where one class has learned to read using ita. When the test results are examined it is found that the children who learned to read using ita have a higher average mark than the children in the other classes. Would it be reasonable in these circumstances to say that to learn to read with ita was better than to learn by the other methods used? Unless the conditions were controlled no such assumption could be made. Without control, it could be that the teacher using ita was a better teacher than the others, that she had a smaller class, that her class spent more time on reading, that the children were more intelligent than those in other classes and so on. Before any useful comparison can be made an *experimental group* must be matched with a *control group*. If evidence is required about the efficacy of ita then it must be collected by a comparison of two such groups – the experimental group learning by ita and the control group learning by traditional methods. The groups would need to be made up of equal numbers of children who, on entering school, are matched for age, home background, health and performance on suitable tests of learning ability. These two groups must then be given the same learning conditions and their teachers should be as alike as possible and equally interested in the collection of the evidence. Then, and only then, will it be appropriate to measure the results of the two groups with a view to gathering evidence about the benefits of ita. Even when the marks of two such groups are compared, a higher average for the experimental group will not necessarily mean that ita is beneficial. There are statistical methods by which it must be determined whether the difference in average mark is small enough to be due to chance or large enough to count as evidence that the experimental group has learned better than the control group. If it is established that the difference is too great to be attributed to chance then the results are said to be significant and can count as evidence (see further reading list, page 11). The reader will recognise that it will frequently be difficult to hold all but one variable constant and there are statistical techniques (not referred to in this book) which in certain circumstances make it possible to consider more than one variable at a time; but the various factors which may influence the outcome and which are not themselves of interest must always be controlled.

It is necessary to think of one further characteristic of scientific study. A scientist does not just observe, experiment and record. He asks questions and when he observes and collects evidence, it is in order to find answers to his questions. '. . . we may collect and classify facts, we may marvel at curiosities and idly wonder what accounts for them, but the activity that is characteristically scientific begins with an explanatory conjecture which at once becomes the subject of an energetic critical analysis' (73, page 154).*

The explanatory conjecture or hypothesis may be thought of as an informed guess which poses a question. It is informed because it arises as a result of previous observations, and it is a questioning guess because in the form, *could it be that* ...? to be followed by the appropriate tests which must be publicly available for checking. Then the process is likely to start again, and it is never finished; scientific knowledge is never certainly true for it is always open to revision in the light of further evidence. The probability of the truth of any statement is estimated by the amount of evidence available for its support. If the evidence justifies a high degree of belief in a proposition it may attain the status of a scientific law, or a number of reasonably probable statements may be accepted and combined to form a theory, to be held until further evidence calls for a revision of the theory.

It is characteristic of new sciences, like psychology, that the amassed evidence does not permit inclusive theories. In this book an attempt has been made to indicate the historical order in which evidence has been collected to support basic learning processes which are described. In order to give explanatory description of these processes anecdotal examples have sometimes been given (e.g. chapter 3, pages 25 ff., motivation of dog Teck). It is most important for readers to recognise that such examples are not given as *evidence* for any hypothesis. They are illustrations for explanatory purposes of processes for which other evidence has been recognised and which may form part of a larger theory. As there is, at present, no widely accepted inclusive theory of learning, no attempt has been made in this introductory book to examine theories (cf. conclusion of chapter 4, page 53).

FURTHER READING

(50), chapter 8, gives a very clear and readable account of the control group and the use of statistics in psychology.

* Numbers in parentheses refer to Bibliography, pages 126 ff.

2 Learning and Behaviour

It is not only men who learn, as anyone knows who has kept a dog, cat, bird or other pet. The ETHOLOGIST in his hide, peering through binoculars at fauna in their natural habitat, and the psychologist in his laboratory, absorbed in the problem solving of rats, pigeons and primates, are each equally interested in *learning*. Ethologists study the adaptive relationships between organisms and their environments. 'The owl for all his feathers is acold' and it fluffs them out, the better to be insulated against the bitter air. Such adaptive changes constitute behaviour which is at once active and reversible. (By contrast, the hydrangea bush battered by the wind is passive and the twining of honeysuckle is irreversible.) Such active, reversible behaviour characterises living beings; and in its most primitive form, as shown, for example, by unicellular organisms, it depends upon what biologists call *irritability*, an unspecialised mechanism for responding to STIMULI. As organisms become increasingly complex, systems of cells become organised to facilitate active, reversible behaviour. These cells form the sense organs and the nervous system. The gradual differential organisation of cells can be seen by an examination of animals from primitive PROTOZOA to PRIMATES. Gradually cells became organised to serve four functions:

(*a*) to detect environmental change both outside and inside the organism;
(*b*) to conduct this information[1];*
(*c*) to integrate the information in preparation for response;
(*d*) to initiate a response.

* Small numbers refer to notes at the end of the chapter.

The behaviour of any organism depends primarily upon the capability of its sense organs and nervous system to carry out these tasks. In vertebrates, the four functions are controlled by the sense organs, which detect as in (*a*), the PERIPHERAL NERVES, to conduct as in (*b*) and (*d*), and the CENTRAL NERVOUS SYSTEM (cns) especially the brain to integrate as in (*c*). Inextricably bound to the evolution of the central nervous system is the development of the ability to learn. At one end of the phylogenetic scale learning has been shown by planarians or flat worms, little creatures ½ to 1 inch long having nerves, muscles and very, very primitive brains (61). At the other end of the scale we have the most complex learning of which man is capable. One may well ask whether it is useful to have one inclusive term, *learning*, to cover such diverse processes as the learning, say, of a planarian, a rat, a child and an Einstein.

THE CONTINUUM OF LEARNING

To answer this question it will be useful to refer to what Hebb (50) has called the procedure of polar definition. 'What the procedure does, really, is to define a continuum by designating its extremes, and then to 'classify' in terms of this *polar definition* by saying that the thing classified is on the continuum, and nearer one pole than the other.' The continuum along which lie all types of learning will be considered in this chapter, but at the outset we must note that learning by different creatures in differing circumstances requires precise description and careful study of differences as well as of similarities. An attempt will be made to provide such description and study later in this book.

We will begin our study of the learning continuum by a consideration of IMPRINTING. This type of learning has only recently been studied in detail but it was referred to, though not named, by Sir Thomas More in *Utopia* (1515) (79).

They (husbandmen) bring up a great multitude of poultry, and that by a marvellous policy. For the hens do not sit upon the eggs but by keeping them in a certain equal heat they bring life into them and hatch them. *The chickens, as soon as they be come out of the shell, follow men and women instead of the hens.*

(My italics)

The last sentence (in italics) describes imprinting.

When a young gosling hatches from an egg it is soon able to walk. This walking is directed, the gosling begins to follow its mother. After the bird has followed its mother for some time it will not follow other animals. But if the egg is hatched in an incubator where there is no mother and if the young gosling is presented with another animal or even with an object, then it will follow that creature or object; and once it has followed this body it will continue to do so and will not subsequently follow a real mother goose. Goslings and other young creatures have learned to follow such objects as moving coloured balloons and blocks of wood as well as a variety of living creatures. You may have seen the much publicised and amusing picture of goslings following Konrad Lorenz, a famous ethologist, because he had intentionally made himself the first creature to be seen by the goslings; and everyone has heard of Mary's little lamb. This type of learning takes place only under certain conditions. Moving objects are preferred and for any species there are size and other limitations to the objects which will be followed. There is also, for any species, a critical period, often of very short duration, during which the learning will take place. If the young bird does not see a suitable object within this period it will not later be able to be imprinted. For example, the period during which a young partridge can be imprinted lasts but a few hours, beginning when the chick is drying off after hatching and ending before it is able to stand (99).

Let us now examine this example of a simple learning process, imprinting, more closely. Immediately upon hatching, the young bird shows a following response. There are various ways of describing this and other similar facts. Some would say that the gosling instinctively follows, others that following is an innate, inbred or inherited action. The most up-to-date description based on present-day knowledge of hereditary mechanisms is to say that following results from genetic information which was provided to the bird's developing nervous system from the code-carrying DNA; or, more shortly, to say that following has been genetically coded or programmed.[2] *Following*, then, is internally programmed, but *what* will be followed is not entirely programmed from within. As we have already seen, limits are set to what will be followed; but between these limits *what* is followed is determined by the young bird's contact with its environment or, to put it another way, what is followed depends upon experience. More fundamentally we may say that what is followed depends upon the information from the outside world[1] transmitted through the nervous system of the young bird. *When*, as in this case, such *transmitted information causes a more or less permanent change in future behaviour*, we say that *learning has taken place*. When our chick's behaviour pattern is complete and he is following a particular body we may say, using current language, that the bird is programmed to follow X, where X is either a natural or an artificial parent figure, and we may say that this total programming is partly due to genetic coding and partly due to learning. *Thus there is no sharp distinction between unlearned and learned behaviour.* (How learning changes the functioning of the cns is not at present fully understood, nor is it certainly known whether there are permanent structural changes in the cns as a result of learning.)

A study of HABITUATION will provide a further illustration of the interaction between unlearned and learned behaviour. The example chosen will concern reactions to danger. Some animals are genetically programmed to avoid very particular stimuli associated with their most dangerous predators. A passing bird of prey excites alarm-calls and escape flight in certain small birds. Experiments by Tinbergen (106) have shown that these responses are made to a *very particular moving pattern*. Birds reared in captivity (who could not have been alarmed by, or learned from, older birds) as well as wild ones, responded to the characteristic, short-necked shape of the bird of prey; but when a model shape was used, the escape flight occurred only when the model was pulled with the short (neck) end in front. When the model was moved in the opposite direction, with the long (tail) end in front, then no avoidance followed. These birds showed a completely fixed or stereotyped reaction and no learning took place. Nevertheless, in some circumstances certain defence mechanisms are subject to change by learning. Thorpe (105) has pointed out that many small defenceless creatures are subject to such a great variety of dangers from so many sources that innate escape responses, tied to specific danger stimuli, would be biologically uneconomic. More advantageously their genetic coding directs them to take avoiding action not to specific stimulus patterns but to classes of stimuli which are likely to signal danger, i.e. to moving objects, and to stimuli which are strange, sudden or of unusually high intensity. They are thus initially on guard against most risks. However, if a potentially dangerous stimulus is frequently repeated and not followed by injury or further disturbance, then gradually the creature will fail to respond with its typical escape pattern. 'Sheep may safely graze' by a railway line and are frequently seen to do so as the hooting Diesel rushes by. The adaptive value of this learning is readily understood. If the animals did not habituate, their lives would be totally taken up with startle responses and escape activities. Men also learn in this way. The human startle response to sudden and loud noises is, for example, fairly rapidly habituated. This is a piece of learning with obvious adaptive advantages in the era of jet planes and supersonic booms.

INTERACTION OF MATURATION, EARLY EXPERIENCE AND LEARNING

As we saw in the case of the signal from the bird of prey, some items of animal behaviour are completely fixed by internal or genetic programming; but the acquisition of most patterns of behaviour depends, as we have seen in the case of imprinting and habituation, upon an interaction between the genetically endowed animal and information received from the environment via its nervous system. It is this interaction which causes the learning, that leads to more or less permanent changes in behaviour, and thus to the possibility of varied behaviour patterns.

Broadly speaking the more simple the nervous system of the creature the more behaviour will be genetically programmed. It is easy to see why this must be so. Poorly developed sensory organs, or a simple nervous system, imply the reception of very limited information from the environment. Such limited information allows for little chance of adaptation to circumstances and action of necessity must be largely ordered from within, and will tend to be rigid and stereotyped. It must be noted that complex sensory organs will not by themselves lead to learning and variability of behaviour. The peripheral nervous system must be sufficiently developed for the information to be carried to the cns, especially the brain. It is, of course, the brain that integrates the separate pieces of information preparatory to action. Hence the most important factor in determining the extent of learning is the degree of brain complexity. When, as in mammals and especially man, sense organs, afferent nerves and brain are all complex, then the information received is vast. It is worth noting, however, that even in man the eye can transform light stimuli into neural energy at such a fast rate that only a small fraction of the information received can be organised by the brain. If, in addition, efferent nerves and EFFECTORS, as well as RECEPTORS, sense organs and brain are complex, which is especially the case for monkeys, apes and men, then the possibility of variable adaptive behaviour is maximised and, as would be expected, programming from outside, or learning, becomes far more important than internal or genetic programming and fixed behaviour patterns. In men it is almost impossible to find behaviour where genetic programming is not, or cannot be, affected by learning. This is not to say, however, that genetic programming is unimportant. It provides the basic REFLEXES, such as the startle response already mentioned, and in addition it controls the growth of the whole body, including the nervous system. This maturational growth is responsible for the successive appearance of capacities for learning. In the gosling, internal programming made the chick able to walk and capable of following. In human beings internal programming, as maturation, gradually increases capacity to learn. Thus children can develop in ways which are studied in courses on child development and which will not be elaborated here (70).

Nowhere is the close interaction of inherited or genetically controlled ability and ability resulting from experience more

B

clearly shown than in the early development of young creatures, including the human infant.

This interaction can be studied by rearing young animals in abnormal conditions, and revealing experiments of this kind have been carried out when investigating the manner in which perceptual skill is acquired. When young chimpanzees are reared in the dark for the period of either 0–16 months or 8–24 months there is some degeneration of the neural connections between the retina of their eyes and their brains (92). Kittens have been reared with only one eye deprived of the normal visual field. The eye cover may be opaque, thus preventing all light from reaching the eye, or it may be translucent, so that though diffuse light reaches the eye there is no patterning of light stimuli (57). Unlike the chimps, in neither case do the kittens show any degeneration of cells. Nevertheless, in both cases certain neural connections, known to function at birth and still functioning from the un-shaded eye, do not now function from the deprived eye. Appropriate experience is thus shown to be necessary, at least in infancy, for the maintenance of neural structure and function originally present as a result of genetic constitution.

There is also evidence that under normal conditions much *learning* goes on during the early months and years of life which affects later abilities. In our own culture few of us have much difficulty in distinguishing one from another the individuals with whom we come into contact. But it is a common experience for Europeans to find it, at first, very difficult to distinguish one Oriental face from another, and vice versa. Such a difference in perceptual ability must be due to early learning through practice. Effects of early learning are even more noticeable in the case of auditory perception and performance. In their early babbling, babies all over the world produce the *same sounds* in the same maturational order. Most people find this surprising and foreign language teachers, when told this, are frankly incredulous. In England, French teachers cannot credit that their pupils once pronounced French nasals with ease; while their colleagues teaching German are astounded to know that the pupils once correctly produced German vowel sounds. Elsewhere, of course, there is the opposite circumstance. French and German children beginning to learn

English can no longer produce sounds characteristic of the English language. Babies quickly begin to practise sounds which they frequently hear and which are rewarded because meaningful. Much behaviour of human children, like that of other creatures, is adaptive and, to use an Americanism current among some psychologists, children learn what 'pays-off'. To use another Americanism, the genetic ability which is unprofitable tends to 'drop-out'.

In experimental conditions it may be possible to separate the effects of genetic maturation from those of early learning, but practically this is both difficult and unnecessary. It is better to separate the influences on the development of behaviour into constant and variable factors. Two important constant factors which are, in practice, inseparable are the genetic factor and the sensory constant factor, where this is defined as early experience which is normally inevitable. The recognition of the importance of early learning experience has led to an important reappraisal of the concept of readiness for learning in school. In the past there has been some considerable tendency to equate *readiness* with *maturation*, but the obvious importance of almost inevitable sensory experiences in very early learning has led to the reasonable supposition that the richness of environmental experience throughout childhood may complement chronological development in producing readiness for later learning. We shall return to this extended concept of readiness in later chapters.

CONCLUSION

We are now in a better position to consider the continuum of learning. Some writers have suggested as opposing limits, simple learning in worms and complex learning in man, the learning of other species being ranged along the continuum in the evolutionary order of the animal families. It is true that as species are thus ordered there is a gradual rise in the dominance of learned behaviour over other types of behaviour. But this suggested continuum is not entirely satisfactory, for as we have already shown, men as well as flat-worms, small mammals, etc., learn by the relatively simple process of habituation, even though they also learn in more complex ways. In another context Munn has written (83), 'There are no learning processes which are unique in children as opposed to animals and adults'. Some students of behaviour have tried to estimate the proportion to which any piece of behaviour owes its origin to genetic and learned factors respectively. The continuum then suggested is a behavioural one, the limits being completely stereotyped behaviour at one end and the sophisticated problem solving of intelligent and educated men at the other. This is again not a satisfactory continuum, for it has already been shown that there is no sharp distinction between learned and unlearned behaviour and that it is extremely difficult to separate the two influences in early life; while the puzzle over the origin of the intelligence necessary for complex problem solving is too well known to call for further remark. Both of these attempts to define a continuum of learning, though unsatisfactory, have been tied to points made in this chapter, namely the connection between the evolution of the nervous system and learning and the interaction of unlearned and learned behaviour patterns. To find a more satisfactory way of defining the continuum we may look at a further point which has been made.

The earliest attempt to describe learning in this chapter ran as follows: when information transmitted by the nervous system from the outside world causes a more or less permanent change in future behaviour, then *learning* has taken place. This provisional description of learning can point a way for delineating a continuum of learning. It can provide a criterion for ordering the various known learning processes: imprinting, habituation and those to be described in later chapters. The question to be asked when ordering the processes will be 'How much transmitted information is required for this type of learning to take place?' In the event, this information may have come immediately from the outside environment or be available as a result of previous learning. In the latter case the information would be remembered as a result of a storage system in the cns. (This system will be considered in a later chapter, though we may note here that the method of storage is a matter of some knowledge and considerable speculation.) It is not difficult to find appropriate limits for the continuum under discussion. Imprinting is well placed at one end, for the only information used in this process is the single sight of one figure. At the other end will be placed complex problem solving where all relevant information from past and present experience must be marshalled to provide a solution. It may, perhaps, occur to some to ask whether problem solving is a genuine process of learning. Quite clearly it is, for the solution of problems of a certain kind makes it easier to solve problems of a similar, but not identical, type. That this is so will become clear to the reader if he reflects upon his own past learning in, say, mathematics or one of the sciences. Although it will be considered later in some detail, it must here be noted that many teaching methods rest on the assumption that learning to solve problems is in itself a useful skill. Habituation can result from few presentations of very simple stimuli, in which case little information is involved. For this reason it will be placed next to imprinting along the continuum. But possible differences between various instances of habituation must be considered. When birds cease to fly away at the intermittent explosions of a mechanical scarecrow, learning has been the result of repetitions of a single piece of information. Suppose now that we are considering the deaf ear of the harassed husband and the sullen indifference of his perpetually scolded daughter. Both father and child have become habituated to the strident tones of this nagging wife and mother, but the repeated information is far more complex than that received by the birds. Nevertheless, habituation to the nagging tones is a more simple process than learning to deal with it by understanding the attitude of the speaker and the content of the spoken messages. In ordering the various types of learning along the chosen continuum we must recognise that each type covers a broad band of experiences and that in consequence complex forms of one type may overlap simple forms of the next. For example, the second instance of habituation given above may be further along the continuum than a simple example of classical conditioning which will be the next process to be considered. In recognising this fact we are observing the dictum, stated earlier, that learning by different creatures in differing circumstances requires precise description and careful study.

SUMMARY

All organisms have a genetic constitution and they live in an environment from which they receive information and in which they act. Creatures transform energy from stimulus objects into neural energy and thus receive coded information from the world. If the receipt and organisation of this coded information in the brain leads to the possibility of more or less permanent changes in the creature's behaviour then learning has taken place. The extent to which this process can be carried out depends on the complexity of the animal's nervous system. Ability to learn implies variability of behaviour. In this book, the criterion for ordering learning processes for description and study will be according to the amount of information organised to bring about a specific change in behaviour.

NOTES

1. *Stimulus objects, the nervous system and information*
   The unsophisticated say that we see X or touch Y, etc., and there is no problem, for they do not enquire into the manner by which the transition is made from the outside world through the senses to the brain. The sophisticated say that energy emitted by stimulus objects is transformed into nervous energy to give information to the brain. Some examples will serve to show how the word *information* is used in this biological sense, which is rather different from its everyday use and from its use by communication engineers.

   A spider is informed that prey is in the web by feeling vibrations through the thread, sometimes a very long one, which connects the web with the spider in its lair. Some parasitic animals, such as ticks, locate their warm-blooded hosts by sensing the higher temperature of the air surrounding the host's body. Fish have taste buds all over their bodies, while we have them only on our tongues, and experiments have shown that minnows can detect the presence of minute quantities of sugar in solution. They are much better at gaining information about the strength of sugar solutions than men. It is estimated that they are about sixty times better. A dog tracks both friend and enemy by detecting their scent with his nose. A cat is informed of the mouse behind the skirting-board long before the householder. Indeed, it may be the sight of the pricked ear, the twitching whisker and the crouched position of puss, which informs the human of the rodent's hide-out.

In every case, these living creatures are detecting the physical and chemical make-up of their environment by means of their sensory equipment and a selectively sensitive nervous structure, which enables them to transform energy emitted by stimulus objects into neural energy. The energy from the stimuli may be mechanical (e.g. vibrations), electro-magnetic (e.g. light), or chemical (e.g. particles affecting taste and smell). Transformed into neural energy it becomes a coded message to the brain. At the present time, attempts are being made to explain the transmission of this code by analogy with the work of communication engineers working on electronic transference of messages. These explanations are beyond the scope of this note.

It is worth noting that for some creatures there are second order stimuli which represent features of the universe. Man is best able to deal with such symbolic material chiefly represented by language, pictures, models, etc. Dealing with these symbols is sometimes referred to as operating *the second signalling system*. The method of receiving neural information is similar in all nervous systems, but it is the extent and complexity of the information which differs from one species to another. The degree to which resultant brain activity implies consciousness in species other than man is a matter of conjecture, but the connection between sensory reception, consciousness and thought in man, has been well recognised for centuries. 'There is no conception in man's mind, which hath not at first, totally, or by parts, been begotten upon the organs of sense' (Thomas Hobbes 1588–1679).

2. As a result of his well-known work on the hybridisation of peas, Gregor Mendel (1822–1884) inferred the existence of a large number of independent inheritable units. Not until 1902 was it suggested that the CHROMOSOMES might contain these units, and not until the 1920s were they named as genes which could be located in definite positions on the chromosomes. Another twenty years elapsed before it was recognised that the long-sought raw material of heredity was a substance found only in chromosomes, deoxyribonucleic acid (DNA). By 1952, not only were the components of DNA known but also it was possible to make a model of its molecular structure. As there was nothing unusual about the components – phosphates, sugars and bases containing nitrogen – it was recognised that its uniqueness must lie in its structure and hence the importance of the model. This model suggests that a molecule of DNA is made up of two intertwined spirals connected to each other by thousands of pieces of material so that the whole is like a long narrow twisted ladder. This whole is built of pairs of units called nucleotides. A nucleotide contains sugar and phosphate which form one side of the spiral ladder and a base which forms half a

rung. The sugar and phosphate of a paired nucleotide form the other side of the spiral and its base joins with the partner base to complete the rung.

There are four different bases, frequently designated by their initials A, G, T, C. A and T are always paired together as are G and C. Thus the rungs on the long spiral ladder might be arranged

$$A \quad A \quad G \quad A \quad C \quad T$$
$$| \quad | \quad | \quad | \quad | \quad |$$
$$T \quad T \quad C \quad T \quad G \quad A$$

and so on. Each molecule will, therefore, have its own distinctive sequence of these sub-units. It is these sequences which determine the characteristics of species and individuals carrying them. The number of sequences in which four such pairs can be arranged when there are millions of pairs is calculated to be more than enough for the variety of genetic properties which they have to determine. The method by which these units are passed from parent to offspring and the way in which they control cell development in individuals (page 14) is beyond the scope of this note. (See list of books for further reading.)

FURTHER READING

The 'Life Science and Nature Libraries' are attractive and readable series (66) (67) and will be useful to amplify Note 2. In this connection Darlington (26) and Riley (94) will also be interesting. Other suitable supplementary reading is Barnett (6), Broadhurst (15), Foss (35), Lowenstein (71) and Milne (78).

3 Motivation and Learning

Selective behaviour

Psychology has been informally described as 'the study of what makes people tick' but the phrase better describes the study of MOTIVATION.

One morning, on four successive occasions, dog Teck is observed going into the garden. The first time he jumps over the water trough, ignores the birds at the end of the lawn and cocks his leg beside the tree stump. The second time he drinks from the trough. The third time he dashes round the tree stump and down the garden to chase birds. The last time he picks up the ball which has been lying by the trough, drops it on the doorstep, barks and, ignoring the startled birds, continues to bark until I throw the ball; then, circumventing the trough, trunk and other obstacles he runs, jumps and deftly catches the bouncing ball. In the presence of the *same environmental stimuli* what made the dog 'tick' differently on each of his garden excursions? To put it in more psychological language, what caused Teck to be active in a selective, organised way? In other words, what motivated Teck?

Drives and arousal

It is reasonable to say that he cocked his leg and urinated in order to relieve bladder tension and that he drank because he was thirsty. This account suggests that DRIVES to reduce physiological tensions or to satisfy basic biological needs will determine some examples of selective behaviour, and this is indeed the case. During the past thirty to forty years, steady progress has been made in understanding the operation of drives which function in this way. In the 'thirties, theories relating to such systems of motivation were known as HOMEOSTATIC theories and, since the 'fifties, similar motivational theories have been spoken of in the language used to describe SERVOMECHANISMS (see further reading list, page 37). As so often happens in science, these theories drew attention to as many problems as they purported to solve and there are still many unsettled issues related to them. In spite of this, some psychologists have demanded that all selective behaviour be accounted for by motivation derived from such drives. 'A tall order' one may say, thinking of the complicated choices which direct one's own selective activities. It is indeed a tall order and one which has been only partially discharged. In the next chapter, we shall see that a stimulus object or situation which is constantly associated with the satisfaction of one of these drives may itself come to satisfy. If this happens, then, in future, this stimulus object or situation may itself act as an INCENTIVE for a selective behaviour pattern. For example, a young widow may take an interest in cricket. She may follow county scores, watch matches on television and visit Lords, simply because these activities become, for her, interesting and pleasurable by association with a loved husband. Here is a case of learned motivation derived, albeit tenuously, from association with the satisfaction of a basic biological drive. Though some motives for action, including some surprising ones, are learned in this way it is now widely recognised that there are other sources of motivation.

Perhaps a further examination of dog Teck's selective behaviour will direct attention to another type of motive. Certainly bird and ball chasing do not appear to relieve tension. On the contrary, the dog, recumbent in the doorway, was much more relaxed than the aggressive bird chaser or the tail wagging barker demanding ball play. Of course, wild dogs give chase for food and the completion of his chasing activities might be supposed to give Teck satisfaction of the kind previously described, but there are two obvious difficulties to this hypothesis. Firstly, the dog was not hungry and, therefore, secondly it is necessary to ask why the behaviour sequences took place when they did. Watching the animal, one was tempted to say that he roused himself and looked about for something to do. In view of other evidence I do not think that this statement is as anthropomorphic as it may sound. We will examine experimental, neurological and ethological evidence concerning this motivational problem.

Some relevant evidence has come from well-known experiments carried out by R. A. Butler and his associates (21). Butler placed rhesus monkeys each in a dimly lit box. The box had two windows covered with yellow and blue shutters respectively. The yellow shutter was locked, but the blue shutter was hinged so that the monkey could push it open. The animal was then able for 30 seconds to view the scene outside before the door swung to. The monkeys not only quickly learned to open the shutter in order to be rewarded by viewing, but also showed remarkably little satiation. That is to say, the experience of viewing did not seem to be like the appetitive behaviour associated with the fulfilment of the biological needs so far considered. Rather the monkeys behaved '. . . as if increase of appetite had grown by what it fed on . . .'. In another experiment, Butler (22) deprived monkeys of visual experience for periods of 0, 2, 4, and 8 hours, and rewarded them with a 12-second sight of other monkeys. The rewarding response increased in frequency according to the length of deprivation time up to 4 hours.

It will be easier to see the significance of these experiments when we have considered neurological work, for recently much interest has been shown in the arousal or vigilance function of the brain. Progress in the study of this, and other brain activities, has been facilitated by recent advances in methods of recording the change in potential of electrical impulses in the CORTEX (see further reading on ELECTROENCEPHALOGRAPHY, EEG (8, 111)). In the last chapter it was made clear that stimuli provide the brain with items of information. These items may be regarded as cues for action and after suitable organisation by the brain, action takes place. However, stimuli will only act as cues for action if the recipient is alert. Recent work suggests that alertness or vigilance depends upon activation of a system of nerve fibres known as the reticular formation. It appears that stimuli *first* arouse by activating this system and *then* give information which leads to action. The reticular formation of nerve fibres controls sleeping and waking. In sleep there is minimal arousal. Maximal arousal occurs as a result of subjection to very many stimuli of high intensity. The response to such intense arousal is strong emotion which tends to prevent or disorganise action. Consider the following homely example of the disruptive effects of simultaneous stimuli of high intensity. Next door the radio blares, baby is screaming, the phone ringing, the milk boiling over and now someone bangs the door knocker. The young mother, near to tears, makes frantic starts between stove, door, phone and baby, but reaches nowhere. It is characteristic of arousal that between quiescence and disruptive emotion the degree of alertness or vigilance determines the efficiency of the brain in analysing and integrating the coded messages from cue stimuli. Later, in chapter 8 (page 116), we shall think about optimum degrees of arousal for particular learning tasks, but at present we will consider arousal in relation to exploration.

Animals in the wild explore their home territories. This exploration is not to be confused with the goings and comings of food gathering, mating, nest building, etc., though the information gained through exploration will obviously affect such activities (72). That exploration can be distinguished from the appetitive behaviour already mentioned has been shown both by experiments with laboratory rats and by watching wild rats placed in a large area of new territory (5). It has, for example, been observed that laboratory rats upon waking will eat and drink their fill, relieve themselves and then begin to explore. (Perhaps there is a parallel here with human tourists who, arriving in a famed city, first find a restaurant and then see the sights!) Hebb (50) has given a tentative account along the following lines of how the arousal system operates in controlling exploratory behaviour. Owing to habituation (page 15) the stimuli of a well-known area have ceased to have an arousing function, but as soon as the animal moves to newer regions stimuli exert this function, the animal becomes vigilant and stimuli can now begin to exert cue function. Simultaneously, innate mechanisms of withdrawal from strange and intense stimuli will come into action (page 16) and be accompanied by fear. We know fear at first hand and can recognise it in other creatures by overt signs and by measuring its physiological symptoms such as rate of breathing, pulse rate, chemicals released into blood stream, etc. Although the appropriate reaction to strange and intense stimuli is flight, intense fear may either immobilise, as described in the expression 'petrified by fear', or cause disorganised panic action. In either case, as with other intense emotions, the normal pattern of selective action is disrupted and stimuli can no longer be informational. Exploratory behaviour, therefore, may in extreme circumstances cease or end in panic, but usually progress or retreat is determined by the dominance of arousal by novelty or withdrawal through fear. An account of rat behaviour written in 1899 (100) describes rats restlessly poking and smelling, advancing here and withdrawing there, as showing 'premonitions of curiosity' and writing in 1966 Hebb (50) said, 'There are times . . . when an animal has no threat to escape, no need of food and no young to care for, no sexual motivation and no need of sleep. One need remains: to be active, physically and mentally'. This need leads to exploration and a search for activity for its own sake. Some name the drive towards the fulfilment of this need GENERAL DRIVE and some call the activities which accompany exploration, play. Exploration and play are important occasions of learning. This study of the evidence for arousal and exploration should make it possible to account for the occurrence and motivation of the dog Teck's last two garden sorties. He had been dormant (near sleep) and-thus receiving very limited arousal stimuli. (His reticular formation was not very actively carrying the sensory messages of arousal.) Like the deprived rhesus monkeys who needed stimulation and worked for it, Teck prepared by getting up. Like the satiated, but exploratory, rats he was ready for action. Genetic programming made it possible for him to chase and he chased birds to be active in play. With a ball and practice, both provided by his master, chasing play had already become skilled ball play, and now he demanded ball games 'for fun'. Man carries exploration further into the realm of symbolic material or second order stimuli, the stuff of thought. The 'premonitions of curiosity' become curiosity, which may be thought of as general drive towards cognitive activity. Along the evolutionary line there is a gradual transition from a predominance of activity which is mainly muscular (though of course it requires elaborate neural control, as in Teck's ball play) to a predominance of activity which principally requires thinking and problem-solving. In some creatures transitional occupations requiring both forms of activity are observed with clarity. Chimpanzees will solve, with no reward other than satisfactory solution, manipulatory puzzles which require the minimum of muscular effort but considerable 'understanding' of the mechanism of the locks, hinges, etc. Further, they have learned to solve problems which, when solved by men, are regarded as involving thought and the use of concepts. For example, apes have been trained to pick the odd one from a variety of trios (46).

That cognitive activity, no less than other activity, depends upon the presence of arousing stimuli is shown by the following experiment (11).

Students were offered a very well-paid job. They were to earn twenty dollars a day which was more than they were likely to get elsewhere. When the nature of the job was known there was a rush to sign up, for the students were to get their pay for doing nothing, absolutely nothing. Each student lay for 24 hours a day on a comfortable bed in a bare compartment which was kept at a comfortable, even temperature. Earphones kept sound at a constant but subdued hum. A translucent shield was worn over the eyes and plastic cuffs were put over hands and wrists to minimise touch stimuli. The only breaks were for very short intervals to eat and use the toilet. At first students slept, but after this they were only able for a very short time to stand these conditions, which they found most distressing. At first they warded off the stress by thinking about things which interested them. Some tried to solve problems, but very quickly they found that they could not concentrate and could not sustain even a simple train of thought. This was, to most, the worst feature of the situation and some reported hallucination. Although they had been asked to keep the job for as long as possible, most students stayed for no longer than two or three days. Although they were short of money they preferred to work hard for much less cash, rather than endure such *sensory deprivation* which prevented the essential activity of thinking.

MOTIVATION FOR LEARNING

Boredom is the name given to lack of arousal, where not only is no action possible but also there is no possibility of sustained and interesting thought sequences. The extreme boredom of experimental perceptual isolation, or of some pathological states leading to the isolation of the insane, occurs rarely; but varying degrees of boredom are known by all of us. It is the enemy of learning, simply because it reduces the possibility of active sustained thought. It is a challenge to teachers, though, of course, it is not the only challenge. Happy the teacher when every pupil is hard at work, happier still if every pupil is totally absorbed in enjoyable learning. Even among good teachers there are few who have never felt frustrated at their pupils' rejection of some potentially interesting work. What makes a person start to learn X but be unwilling to learn Y? What keeps a person at the task, once he has begun? These are questions about motivation for learning. To come to terms with them it may help the reader to consider his present motives for learning the content of this book.

I hope that some are reading with understanding and endeavouring to remember because they are *genuinely interested* in the topics under discussion. But there are no doubt some who are attentively trying to learn only, or at least partly, because they have an essay to write, an assignment to prepare or an examination to pass, and they wish to *perform these tasks well*. If this is the case some students will wish to do well because they *have set themselves standards* and they want *self-approval*. Some students may be more concerned about the opinions of others, and they want the *approval* of their tutors, *recognition* from their fellow students or perhaps they want to do well *in order to please*, or at least *not to disappoint*, their parents. Yet others may have their eye fixed only on a final certificate or degree followed by the *salary and status* of a teacher (even if these at present are far from princely!). This last category of readers may be hurriedly scanning pages without interest, simply to remember the minimum for the shortest time necessary to achieve their immediate object. Motives for learning are not, of course, mutually exclusive and students may recognise that in some measure they are influenced by each of the separate motives, operating together. Indeed, this is very probable for, to parody Oscar Wilde, motivation for learning, like truth, is never pure and rarely simple. Neither is motivation *static*. I should feel flattered to know that some students began to read this book from duty and continued from interest, though the reverse may happen and the student become *bored*. Further, what happens while this book is read will *change attitudes and interests* and affect the motivation for reading other books on similar topics. There is also another complication. The student who has to hand in an essay at the end of the month may find it very difficult to read at the beginning of the month. He finds it difficult to work unless there is more *urgency* about the task. Alternatively, if he leaves the reading until the night before the test, he may then be in such a state of *anxiety*, or near-panic, that he cannot learn even though he is *feverishly active* and trying to do so (page 28).

The italicised words in the above paragraph will guide further discussion on motivation for learning.

Genuine interest

In the first section of this chapter it has been recognised that living creatures actively explore and that man extends this exploration to thought. At the intellectual level, curiosity leads to a search for knowledge and understanding by the process of argument and problem solving. To say, then, that one is reading or learning with genuine interest is to say that one is motivated by curiosity or the desire for mental exploration. One is following a line of argument, asking one's own questions and trying to *integrate the new knowledge with past experience and learning*. At the level of scholarly research this is what advances the frontiers of knowledge. It may not be fanciful to suggest that sustained interest is the intellectual parallel of the emotionally toned alternation of advance and retreat shown in physical exploration. It is to use this powerful form of motivation that discovery methods of learning and teaching are introduced into schools and these will be considered later.

It can escape the notice of only the least perceptive, that individuals differ in the extent to which they show lively curiosity.

The origin of these differences is complex and properly belongs to a study of individual development which lies outside the scope of this book (see page 17) but we are interested in learning conditions which will maximise and develop any individual's capacity for active enquiry. The important effect of early experience upon later learning was mentioned in the last chapter and it has an equally important effect upon motivation. An examination of the conditions of early experience which promote adventurous curiosity may point the way for later provision of conditions for adequate motivation. Many investigations have been made of the mother–child relationship. That there is much controversy about its nature and importance is in part because, in the study of this relationship, there are so many uncontrollable variables. Human mothers will not usually agree that their children shall be reared under controlled conditions or deprived for experimental purposes! (page 9). But, in spite of arguments about the origin, growth and importance of the relationship, there is general agreement that for satisfactory development an infant does need soft, comfortable, tactile stimuli and that these are normally provided by a mother or mother figure (cf. page 50). C. T. Morgan (80) states that the affectional object (the one providing the comfortable stimuli), namely the mother or mother figure, allays fear in strange situations, provides a feeling of security and supports curiosity. As evidence for this statement he cites work by H. Harlow (47) with rhesus monkeys. Though Harlow's work was not designed to study conditions supporting curiosity, Morgan's use of evidence from part of Harlow's work seems justified. The monkeys had been reared with mother surrogates which were wire figures covered by terry cloth. The monkeys showed their attachment to the figures by spending most of their time clinging to them irrespective of whether or not they sucked milk from a bottle attached to the 'mother'. In a series of tests the infant monkeys were placed in a room with a number of strange objects. The presence or absence of 'mother' in the room made a great difference to the child's behaviour. In her absence the monkeys showed acute fear and screamed in distress. When the mother figure was present the little animal rushed to it, clung to it, rubbed against it and then peered out at

c

the strange 'world'. Soon he left the mother, ran a little distance, touched or picked up an object and then quickly returned to 'mum'. This process was repeated, the sorties becoming longer and the activity more venturesome until the refuge was barely required. This controlled experimental situation is, of course, supported by everyday observation. Who has not seen a toddler cautiously advancing towards the new, with many a backward glance at Mum or Dad? It may as yet be an unproven assumption that the quality of this early relationship affects an individual's later manifestation of curiosity but in this context the point is irrelevant. Our interest in Harlow's evidence is that it suggests conditions for learning which will encourage enquiry. It supports the experience of many practising teachers that children are more ready to attack learning in an enquiring and confident way if they can work from a secure setting. The most important factor in this setting will be a stable sympathetic teacher and this is especially true for young children. But support, especially in the middle years of childhood, is also derived from settled practice, regular routine and known regulations. Such a background is likely to promote the best conditions for children to use their varying degrees of adventurous curiosity. It is not, of course, enough to supply such security. There must, in addition, be varied and exciting material to explore. No amount of benevolent stability will make up for paucity of stimulation; alone, settled routines will bring boredom. Another most important point must be made. It may be that the worst learning conditions occur when either regulations have become ends in themselves or when the teacher (or parent), enjoying the position of trusted figure, has encouraged children to remain dependent, so that they cannot venture on their own (42). When learning is undertaken to satisfy a learner's own curiosity his learning is said to be intrinsically motivated, that is, there is no external reward or incentive. The activity is carried on for its own sake.

A look back to pages 31 and 32 will show that learning may be extrinsically motivated, that is, the learner may work for a reward additional to the skill or knowledge to be acquired.

Social motivation for learning
The learner who wants approval and recognition from others is socially motivated. It is obvious that such motivation implies an existing relationship between the learner and those whom he wishes to please. To any learning situation, a socially motivated learner brings a set of attitudes which determine whom he will aim to impress. The characteristics of this admired person will determine what the learner will consider worthy of his attention. Too often, teachers have assumed that it is they whom youngsters wish to please and that the youngsters know automatically what it is that will please. It is probable that a young child will want to please a teacher (see page 50) and that he will be willing to learn the customs, habits, skills and knowledge offered, even though some of these may be at variance with his home background. For older pupils it may be different. Recently, sociologists interested in education have studied the effects of varying home and social backgrounds upon motivation for learning (see reading list, page 37). It is important that teachers shall come to know these studies, for if they have known different social and educational backgrounds from their pupils they may be surprised and enlightened. They may find that they can better appreciate what formerly appeared as inexplicable vagaries in learners' interests and standards, and they will better understand a particular learner's peer group and his need for recognition by his peers. This is not to say that teachers must necessarily accept the individual evaluations of their pupils. A youngster's attitudes have been acquired through social contacts and the process is not static. The teacher is one of many able to influence, and an understanding of the youngster's viewpoint is the first step towards mutual understanding, appreciation and perhaps compromise.

To some extent the operation of social motives is a circular one. Most school-children, like most human beings, enjoy praise; if the teacher gives it, the learner responds with goodwill, rapport is established and the learner is more ready to accept standards from the teacher (cf. chapter 8, page 116). The ease with which rapport is established will partly depend upon the personality of the teacher, but it will also depend upon each child's previous experience. Those who have enjoyed happy contacts with adults will respond more quickly than those who have had less fortunate contacts (cf. page 50). To refer to our earlier example, the students who wished to please their parents and satisfy their tutors had probably previously had amicable and helpful guidance at home and at school. A student who has developed his own work habits and standards and is now able to act as his own best judge and fair critic, has reached an important stage of maturity. It does not necessarily mean that he no longer needs approval and recognition from seniors and peers, but it does mean that he can learn and work independently. Teachers can give praise as well as external rewards (analogous to the salary and status mentioned in the case of student teachers) to train and further this development of self-set standards (cf. page 119). This process of training is, however, a complex one. For its understanding it is necessary to know more about learning processes and we will return to achievement motivation in a later chapter.

SUMMARY

Part One
Stimuli objects or events have two functions. They arouse the brain to activity and they supply the brain with coded information. The information is used selectively, to reduce tension derived from un-satisfied needs, and to explore. The general drive to explore and be active, both physically and mentally, is a chief source of learning. Of the 'What is it?' investigating or orientating reaction Pavlov wrote, it is '. . . the parent of that scientific method through which we hope one day to come to a true orientation in knowledge of the world around us' (88).
Examples. 'Mummy, what can I do now?', 'Daddy, why is . . .?'
Mallory climbed the mountain because it was there.
Technician: 'That's sewn up, now what shall we make?'
Scientist: 'Yes, that's so, but how to explain . . .?'
Theoretician: 'That being so, what follows?'
Bored: 'Arouse me! Turn up the record-player, pass me the hemp or the hypodermic.'

Part Two
Optimum conditions for intrinsically motivated learning: a stable background in a richly varied environment.

Optimum conditions for socially motivated learning: a teacher, with social awareness and goodwill, who can establish rapport with individuals and groups, and so be able to set standards.

Achievement motivation will be discussed in a later chapter.

FURTHER READING

Murray (84) should prove an interesting supplement to this chapter. Miller (76), chapter 16 should give an understanding of homeostasis and put it into historical perspective. Bayliss (8) though difficult, interprets biological systems in terms of servomechanisms. Walter (111) is a fascinating account of EEG. Fowler (36) deals with the whole problem of curiosity and exploration and contains a selection of readings on this topic. Students interested in sensory deprivation will find Vernon (110) very readable. Harlow's work with baby monkeys is well summarised in Harlow (48). Students wishing to follow up the suggestion on page 35 will find the following useful. Argyle (3, chapters 2 and 9), Craft (24), Evans (31) and Stenhouse (102). Students particularly interested in the education of boys may find Hargreaves (44) and Wilmott (114) interesting.

4 Classical Conditioning and Basic Learning Processes

Animals behave selectively and in most cases their behaviour is closely linked with learning. For example, simple explorative behaviour shows the effect of past habituation and is the source of new learning about the environment. At a more sophisticated level consider the photographer. He may have learned well how to operate his equipment, and this knowledge will be used whenever he takes a photograph, but on each occasion he may acquire greater skill in composing pictures, becoming more aware of balance, focal point, colour harmonies, and so forth. Thus at any given time behaviour may at once show the effects of past learning and be the occasion for new learning. This fact has led to difficulty in studying learning processes. Upon examination of any particular piece of behaviour the student of learning is likely to find himself asking questions of the following kind. 'What exactly am I supposed to be studying?' 'Which piece of this complex pattern of behaviour will give me information about learning which is going on now?' 'How can I separate from this total behaviour pattern the processes which are leading to new learning?' This intricacy has caused students from the earliest times to seek some basic feature or features of all learning which can, as it were, be located in complex situations.

ASSOCIATION

Aristotle (384–322 B.C.) was perhaps the first to look for such a basic process. To explain remembering he put forward a principle (4) which later came to be known as the association of ideas. According to this principle the occurrence of one idea will lead to the recall of another; if the two have previously been presented together, if they are similar to each other, or conversely if they are in direct contrast to each other. *Idea* is not a precise term and association of ideas is not a precise phrase, but if provisionally we agree that the presentation of a word will give an idea and that the production of a word will represent an idea, then we can test the principle and we find that, on the whole, tests support it (117). For example, almost everybody given the word *thunder* responds with the word *lightning*. These words represent two events always experienced together and therefore presumably the ideas have previously been presented *together*. In our society *knife* frequently brings the response *fork* but it may also lead to *cut* representing an action experienced in conjunction with knife. Many people given a colour word such as red or green respond with a *similar* colour word and in one test 78% of those tested gave *woman* in response to the *opposite, man*.

Philosophers in the nineteenth century supported and extended the principle of association chiefly by reflecting on their own thought processes. But in the latter part of that century psychology began to develop as an experimental science and in 1879 at the University of Leipzig, Wilhelm Wundt established the first psychological laboratory. It was now recognised that it would be essential to study all psychological processes including, of course, association in the controlled conditions necessary to produce public and verifiable evidence (cf. Introduction). The first important study of association to fulfil these conditions was made, however, not by a psychologist but by an eminent Russian physiologist, Ivan P. Pavlov (1849–1936), and his experimental work set the pattern for much future study of simple learning.

PAVLOV'S FIRST EXPERIMENT

While studying the functioning of the digestive glands in dogs, Pavlov had observed some puzzling dog behaviour and, in consequence, at the turn of the century he began his now world-famous experiments which demonstrate the conditions under which association can bring about measurable changes in behaviour. These experiments are fully reported by Pavlov (88) and summarised in many standard textbooks of psychology (80). The interested student should consult these, for here I shall give but a brief outline of Pavlov's work.

The natural or genetically programmed reaction of mammals to food placed in the mouth is the flow from the salivary glands of digestive juice (saliva). But Pavlov in his earlier work had noticed that saliva began to flow when a dog *saw* food, that is, before the food could have been a stimulus for the reflex production of saliva. The capacity to notice importance and relevance is one of many descriptions of genius, and Pavlov was showing this quality when he did not dismiss his observation as trivial but decided to investigate it. He early noticed that the readiness of a dog to salivate in anticipation of food varied according to the conditions surrounding the animal. In order to stabilise these conditions he prepared a loose harness by which the dog could be held in an apparatus set up in a quiet room. Pavlov could now be reasonably sure that the only environmental changes would be those which he introduced as part of the experiment, and later workers have usually taken the same kind of precautions in their experiments. For Pavlov's original experiments one other preparation was necessary. A small operation on one salivary gland of each animal made it possible to collect and measure the saliva flowing from that gland. Now the prepared dog, standing in his loose harness, was presented with food and responded by salivating. Pavlov called the food the unconditional stimulus (UCS), and salivation the unconditional response (UCR). Immediately before the next presentation of food Pavlov sounded a bell. This he called the conditional stimulus (CS). With repetition of this sequence of events the dog began to salivate to the sound of the bell *before* the presentation of food, and finally the dog repeatedly salivated to the sound of the bell in the total absence of food. Such salivation Pavlov called the conditional response (CR), and when the dog consistently made this response he had learned to salivate to the sound of the bell. Learning by this method has come to be known as Pavlovian or Classical Conditioning, and the essential features of the process are:

1. a neutral object or event is presented to a human or animal subject;
2. the response of the subject to the neutral stimulus (CS) is frequently, but not always, the 'What is it?' reaction mentioned on page 36;
3. immediately following the neutral stimulus (CS) comes the presentation of a stimulus to which the subject is known to make a specific response UCS→UCR;
4. after repetitions, the CS produces a response which is the same as, or very similar to, or has the same effect as, the response made to the unconditional stimulus.

The whole process may be represented by a generalised diagram which can be used to illustrate any particular example of classical conditioning.

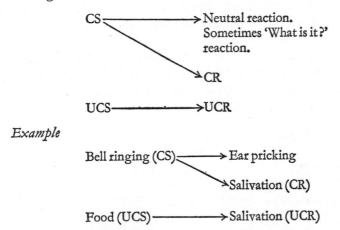

N.B. (1) This diagrammatic form is used for simplicity. The student will remember from note 2 in chapter 2 (page 23) that the stimulus object or event, e.g. food or bell ringing, provides energy which is transformed into neural energy to give coded information to the cns. Transmission of neural energy from cns leads to action.

(2) The adjective *conditioned* traditionally applied in western psychology to stimuli, responses and learning is a mis-translation from Pavlov's writing in Russian. The correct

translation of the adjective used by Pavlov is *conditional* (uslovnii).

There are two reasons why this experiment has been regarded as crucial. Firstly, there was now evidence from *changed behaviour in controlled conditions* that *two events had been associated by near presentation.* Secondly, it opened the way for similar studies which have thrown light on important processes basic to learning.

J. B. WATSON'S EXPERIMENT WITH LITTLE ALBERT (112)

No study of classical conditioning would be complete without a reference to the now famous 'little Albert'. The early behaviourist, J. B. Watson, and his colleague, Rosalie Rayner, in 1920 conditioned the baby boy to fear a white rat. Albert, aged 11 months, when tested before the conditioning procedure showed only two fears. He was afraid of falling and of loud noises. He was not in the least afraid of little furry animals and had played with a white rat and a rabbit for some weeks before conditioning began. There was nothing unusual about the conditioning which can be represented by the following diagram.

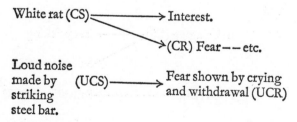

The following extracts from laboratory notes made at the time show how Albert developed the conditional response.

Eleven months, 3 days old

(1) He began to reach for rat with left hand. Just as his hand touched the animal the bar was struck immediately behind his head. The infant jumped violently, and fell forward, burying his face in the mattress. He did not cry, however.

(2) Just as his right hand touched the rat the bar was again struck.

Again the infant jumped violently, fell forward and began to whimper. On account of his disturbed condition no further tests were made for one week.

Eleven months, 10 days old

(1) Rat presented suddenly without sound. There was steady fixation but no tendency at first to reach for it. The rat was then placed nearer, whereupon tentative reaching movements began with the right hand. When the rat nosed the infant's left hand the hand was immediately withdrawn. He started to reach for the head of the animal with the forefinger of his left hand but withdrew it suddenly before contact. *It is thus seen that the two joint stimulations given last week were not without effect.* (my italics)

This entry continues and there are then three records referring to combined stimulation, i.e. presentation of CS and UCS and then:

(5) Rat suddenly presented *alone*. Puckered face, whimpered and withdrew body sharply to left.

There are two more records of combined stimulation and then:

(8) Rat alone. *The instant the rat was shown the baby began to cry. Almost instantly he turned sharply to the left, fell over, raised himself on all fours and began to crawl away so rapidly that he was caught with difficulty before he reached the edge of the mattress.*

Commenting on this record Watson writes,

Surely this proof of the conditioned *origin* of a fear response ... yields an explanatory principle that will account for the enormous complexity in the emotional behaviour of adults. We no longer in accounting for such behaviour have to fall back on heredity.

In the latter half of the nineteen sixties it is difficult to appreciate the novelty of this work and to recognise the force of Watson's comment. On the first page of this book it was emphasised that twentieth-century psychologists attached great importance to *learning* in emotional as well as cognitive development. Watson's work was most influential in bringing about this emphasis and the student of learning must think of poor little Albert as suffering in a good cause. (Watson writes of himself and his colleagues, 'We were rather loath at first to conduct experiments in this field, but the need for study was so great that we finally decided to build up fears in the infant. . . .')

A PRACTICAL APPLICATION OF CLASSICAL CONDITIONING

After looking at these two historically important cases of conditioning it will be as well to look at a present-day practical application of classical conditioning. Enuresis (bed-wetting) is a most disturbing behaviour problem. Practically, even in this whirly-wash age, it disturbs mother; psychologically it is damaging to the child who may feel inferior or guilty or be the butt of thoughtless relatives or friends. A number of children have been cured of this unfortunate habit by what has come to be known as the bell and blanket method of conditional learning. The enuretic, when awake, has normal bladder control but, unlike other children of his age, at night he does not respond to bladder tension by waking. In consequence, urination takes place during sleep. For remedial learning, the child sleeps on an electric blanket so wired that moisture causes the completion of a circuit which triggers a bell. The child is told that when the bell wakes him he should try to control urination, as he can by day, turn off the bell and hurry to the toilet to finish urinating. After a variable number of nights, depending on the individual child, waking occurs without the bell and before urination has begun, and the child gets to the toilet in time. The association between bladder tension and the alarm bell has led waking and control to be associated with bladder tension as well as with the alarm. The conditioning diagram will make the process clear.

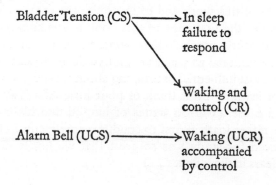

Bladder Tension (CS) ⟶ In sleep failure to respond

⟶ Waking and control (CR)

Alarm Bell (UCS) ⟶ Waking (UCR) accompanied by control

Theoretically, it would be expected that since control is now becoming associated with bladder tension that therefore the child will become capable of retaining urine longer than had previously been possible, and that waking will become less frequent. This has, in fact, been shown to be the case (82). For those who think of such measures as 'newfangled' it is interesting to know that folk-lore preceded experimentation. From parts of West Africa, there are reports of a long standing custom for curing bed-wetting. A certain type of snail is placed on the inside of the thigh of an enuretic. The snail, while dry, is immobile but when wetted it begins to creep and thus serves the same function as the bell (49). Some psychologists, notably Freudians or neo-Freudians, have suggested that to cure enuresis is but to cure a symptom of some more fundamental disorder. Such critics predicted that after cure of this symptom a substitute symptom would appear as an alternative expression of a personality disorder. There is much evidence that this does not usually occur. O. H. and W. M. Mowrer (82) followed up thirty children aged between 3 and 13 years who had been successfully treated and they report

In no case had there been any indication of 'symptom substitution', such personality changes as have resulted from its application being uniformly in a favourable direction. It is concluded that the widespread view that enuresis is always a 'symptom' and must not be dealt with directly represents the misapplication of a concept illicitly borrowed from adult medicine and psycho-pathology.

CONDITIONING IN DAILY LEARNING

Most conditioning takes place in the normal course of daily living and is not especially designed as in the case of laboratory experiments or remedial treatment. In the last chapter we mentioned the wife who, through learning, was motivated to watch cricket. This can now be diagrammed as a typical case of classical conditioning. It has been pointed out (page 40) that for experimental classical conditioning a quiet environment is required. This ensures that the subject's attention is directed to the stimuli to be associated. For the classical conditioning of real life there are

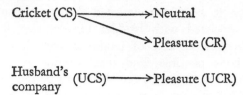

Cricket (CS) ────→ Neutral

────→ Pleasure (CR)

Husband's company (UCS) ────→ Pleasure (UCR)

many stimuli available and the motivation of the individual will determine which of the many stimuli will be paired. For example, in the case just described the pleasure of her husband's company receives more attention or is more important to the woman than, say, the discomfort produced by the hardness of the wooden benches; it is thus the pleasure which becomes the CR and further motivation is effected. The practical effects of classical conditioning can be extensive because in men higher order conditioning is possible.

HIGHER ORDER CONDITIONING

Pavlov's original experiment has been extended. When a dog has learned to salivate to the bell, the bell can be paired with a new stimulus, say a light. If this stimulus, the light, is repeatedly paired with the bell the dog learns to salivate to the light, even if the light has never been paired with food. This process is known as second order conditioning and can be thus diagrammed.

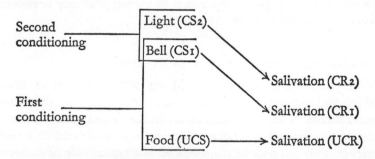

Second conditioning — Light (CS2)

Bell (CS1)

Salivation (CR2)

First conditioning — Salivation (CR1)

Food (UCS) ────→ Salivation (UCR)

As an example of higher (fourth) order conditioning we may take a case of a boy acquiring a dislike of his school. The reader should apply this example to what was said on page 35 about motivation and the example will again be referred to on page 50.

FOURTH ORDER CONDITIONING LEADING TO LEARNED
DISLIKE OF SCHOOL

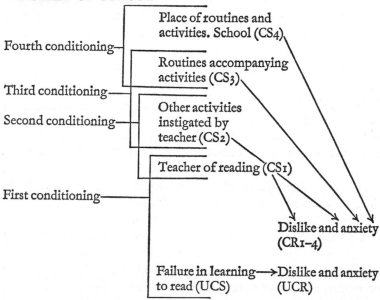

The student should try to think of other such examples of continued or high order conditioning and so the better appreciate Watson's explanatory principle of emotional behaviour (page 43).

The continued experimental study of classical conditioning has brought to light important processes basic to learning and these must now be considered.

EXTINCTION

If, after conditioning, the dog hears the bell, what happens? Repeated bell ringing unaccompanied by food leads to a decrease in the flow of saliva. However, the learned behaviour is not at first permanently changed, for after an interval the animal will again respond to the bell as formerly. Gradually, after intervals between experimental sessions, the dog responds with less and less saliva to the bell and eventually the learned response will fail to appear. Even then the animal is not 'as before', because if the original conditioning procedure is restarted the animal will learn in many fewer trials than were required for the first conditional learning.

The experimental reduction of the effects of conditioning is known as EXTINCTION and in classical conditioning this is brought about by the removal of the UCS.

In ordinary life, when we cannot remember or do something which we have previously learned, we say that we have forgotten. The difference between extinction and forgetting is that the former is brought about by special training while the latter occurs spontaneously. An understanding of extinction will be helpful when studying remembering, forgetting and punishment in later chapters, and further consideration here will relate to child care.

In 1923, three years after conditioning little Albert, J. B. Watson directed attempts to extinguish fears which children had learned in their ordinary lives (112). Peter, aged three years, was afraid of rats, rabbits and other furry and feathery creatures or things. Although Peter's fears had not been artificially conditioned it was argued that, by the principle of extinction, his fear of rats or rabbits should be cured, if the stimulus object (rat or rabbit) could be continuously presented in the absence of any fearful conditioning stimulus. There was, however, a serious practical difficulty. Watson reports, 'At sight of the rat, Peter screamed and fell flat on his back in a paroxysm of fear.' It was clear that the normal conditions required for extinction, namely that the subject shall pay attention to the stimulus, did not exist. After an interval Miss Mary Cover Jones decided to use a rabbit and try, by a process which she called *direct unconditioning*, to cure Peter's fear of it. Miss Jones recognised that the rabbit would only be attended to if Peter was calmly satisfied when he saw it. To rid Peter of his fear she hit on the following plan. While he was having his lunch she put the rabbit inconspicuously in a corner of the forty-foot-long room. With the rabbit at this distance, Peter, although frightened, was not prevented from eating and drinking while casting a wary glance at the animal. Each day the rabbit was brought a little closer until eventually the rabbit could be placed on the table beside Peter without causing alarm. Finally, tolerance of the animal was replaced by positive reactions and Peter would play with the rabbit. There is here a pointer for child care. If a child develops an irrational fear, the wise parent will not insist that there is nothing to be afraid of, confront the child with the feared object or circumstance and thus prevent extinction. Rather she will distract the child and only gradually reintroduce the fearful thing or situation. The principle of allaying fear by the introduction of a pleasurable response (e.g. Peter's lunch) has been called the principle of *reciprocal inhibition*, and an understanding of this principle has led in recent years to important and interesting development in behaviour therapy.[1]

GENERALISATION

Suppose that a dog has learned to salivate to a metronome beating at 80 beats a minute. Will he salivate to a metronome beating at 100 or 60 beats per minute? The answer to this question is, 'Yes', but this does not mean that the animals do not detect the differences, for the responses will be less frequent or less forceful than those given to the original stimulus. Such transfer of a response tendency from one stimulus to another is known as *generalisation*. The fact, for example, that we name a wide range of discriminable colour stimuli *red* is evidence of such generalisation at human level. It will easily be recognised that this process is at the basis of CONCEPT formation and is responsible for much of the acquisition of language. These processes are studied in relation to child development (70) and in a later chapter of this book they will be considered in relation to transfer of learning and problem solving. Our interest here is in generalisation applied to those cases of classical conditioning where the UCR is the expression of an emotion. After conditioning, little Albert was found to fear not only the rat but also a rabbit with which he had formerly played, and many other small furry creatures and objects. Learning as a result of one conditioning experience had been followed by generalisation without the need for further conditioning. Peter, having lost his fear of the rabbit by a process of extinction, was found also to have lost his fear of the rat and other furry objects. He, too, had generalised.

It has already been noted (page 47) that higher order conditioning

D

leads to the spread of emotional reactions and it can now be shown that when this continued pairing of conditional stimuli is followed by generalisation, then the influence of emotional experience becomes even more extensive. Such generalisation may be illustrated by considering the development of a small child's attitude to adults. Although an over-simplification it will not be distorting the essentials to represent the development of a normal, happy relationship between parent and child by the following diagram of second order conditioning (cf. page 33).

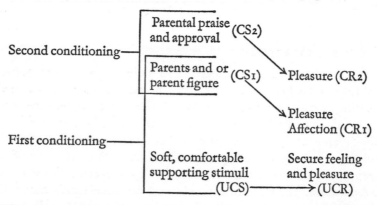

The nineteenth-century psychologist, Alexander Bain, said 'touch is both the alpha and omega of affection' (34, p. 82). If a youngster has developed such a happy relationship with his parents who have encouraged him in, and rewarded him for, co-operative behaviour, then by generalisation he will have to other adults this co-operative attitude (page 36) which stems from a desire to please. To make generalisation from parent to teacher and home to school easy it is necessary to have small informal groups and kindly teachers in the infant school; and this is one reason why emphasis is put on these features of early education. The unfortunate child who has not known affectionate praise from his parents and who has received 'more kicks than ha'pence' will be unlikely to seek help from his teachers, will be unlikely to respond easily and will be as much at a disadvantage in a learning situation as the child who lacks confidence to be curious (cf. page 34).

Let us now follow further the boy who learned by fourth order conditioning to dislike his school (page 47). Suppose now that he gets remedial help, overcomes his reading difficulties and becomes optimistic about his further progress. This sanguine attitude may now be *generalised* to the associated conditional stimuli and not only will his reading improve but his 'school phobia' may be cured. Alternatively, in the absence of help, consider a less happy outcome of this boy's generalisation. Without any experience of other schools the dislike of his own school may be generalised to all schools, to all learning, and perhaps later even to all educated people. Thus, as well as affecting his motivation, generalisation may lead him to prejudice. The pervasiveness of emotional generalisation has been studied experimentally (93) and some studies have shown that there is a good deal of emotional generalisation which accompanies the recognition of word meanings. To illustrate this point we may take the word *conditioning* as an example. As a result of past experiences some people react emotionally to the word and because of their prejudice do not give their usual attention to sentences in which it occurs. Thus, they remain in ignorance of its correct use as a psychological term used when studying learning. Though the evidence is limited it is at least worth asking whether this type of emotional generalisation could account for the surprising irrationality sometimes shown by intelligent and informed people. What for one man is a straightforward argument may for another be charged with emotional overtones brought irrelevantly from the past.

DISCRIMINATION

When the dog, through generalisation, is salivating to the metronome beating at many speeds, he can nevertheless be taught to discriminate between speeds. If the 100 beat per minute ticking is always paired with the food (UCS) and the 80 beat per minute tick is never so paired, then the dog will eventually *discriminate* between the two. That is, in the absence of the UCS he will always salivate to the 100 beat and never to the 80 beat and it is reasonable to say that the two can be differentiated. It is important to consider the effects of presenting learners with discrimination tasks which are too difficult for them. Pavlov and others trained dogs to salivate to lighted circles and not to lighted ellipses. The ellipses were then made wider and wider until they were almost the same as the circles. What happened then? Experimenters report that the dogs became disturbed and disorganised. They salivated at random, sometimes not to the circle, sometimes to even a narrow ellipse. Eventually they just did nothing and withdrew from the task. They had broken down. After a long rest they made some recovery, but it was very difficult to get them to learn anew. So impressed was Pavlov by what he termed the dog's 'experimental neurosis' that he devoted the last years of his life more and more to the study of human neuroses. He recognised, of course, that these were very much more complex than those induced in the dogs, but he put forward the hypothesis that the breakdown in both cases was caused by conflcting reactions in the autonomic nervous system due to the inability to distinguish between a rewarding pleasurable stimulus and a neutral one.[1]

Though it is a far cry from salivating dogs to learning in school, it is possible that there is a parallel between the withdrawal of the dogs from their task and the withdrawal of some children from learning situations. Most teachers are familiar with the child who has 'opted out' and who is extremely, if not impossibly, difficult to motivate. Could some of these children be those who had been given tasks which made too heavy demands upon their powers of discrimination? To ask this question is to point to the need for careful research into causes of poor motivation and to ask in this connection such questions as, 'Do we sometimes ask young children to discriminate between lengths, areas and shapes too soon?', 'Do we know when young children are ready to distinguish between word and letter patterns?', 'Are older pupils sometimes confused by being asked to distinguish between concepts which are too difficult for them?' These are questions which it is proper to ask of developmental and educational psychologists and research workers (see Introduction, page 8), and some similar questions will be referred to later on.

CONCLUSION

It should now be clear that in classical conditioning an S→R connection is made as a result of the near presentation of two sensory stimuli. Associationist philosophers of the nineteenth century were content to talk about the association of ideas derived from sensory stimuli. At the beginning of the twentieth century, emphasis was directed away from this type of association towards the S→R connection because results could be publicly observed. This was very necessary to establish sound evidence for association. Now, growing understanding of the operation of the central nervous system as a transmitter and storer of information has led to greater readiness for, and possibility of, study of internal processes (see page 23). At one time there was a very sharp division between those psychologists ready to consider only S→R connections and those ready to consider associations made internally as a result of S→S connections. This distinction is currently becoming blurred. G. A. Miller writes (76, page 230). 'Many psychologists have broadened their definition of stimulus and response to include unobservable events and processes that play much the same role in their theories as perceptions, images, ideas, and intentions played in the older psychologies.' More will be said in a later chapter about S→S connections and the student interested in different schools of learning and the reconciliation of theories should consult the further reading list (page 55).

Following the recommendation of chapter 1 it must be asked in conclusion, 'How much transmitted information is required for classical conditioning to take place?' In the case of simple conditioning the information is, 'A is accompanied by B'. In cases of higher order conditioning the information may be, 'A is accompanied by B, B by C, C by D' and so on where A represents UCS and B, D, C, etc. represent CS. The total complexity of the information depends, of course, upon the nature of A, B, C, D.

In this chapter, the emphasis has been upon emotional learning, and though not all classical conditioning results in such learning, the most common types of human conditioning involve emotions. Note 1 following this chapter indicates that classical conditioning frequently involves the autonomic nervous system and involuntary responses. Operant conditioning or learning, to be considered in the next chapter, is more concerned with voluntary responses.

A DIAGRAMMATIC SUMMARY OF THE CHAPTER

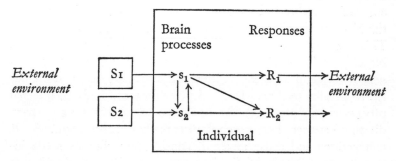

Diagram based on Fig. 3.1, page 74, *Introduction to Psychology* by C. T. Morgan and R. A. King (McGraw-Hill 1966)

NOTES

1. *The Autonomic Nervous System and Classical Conditioning*

The nerves which control and carry messages regulating the heart, glands and smooth muscles of internal organs, make the autonomic nervous system. The name derives from the fact that the operation of these nerves is not under conscious control.

The system is divided into two parts, the sympathetic system and the parasympathetic system. The sympathetic system is activated by stimuli which cause pain or unpleasant excitement such as fear, anger or insecurity. The results of such stimulation are reactions which will aid flight or fight; e.g. relaxing bronchial tension to facilitate rapid breathing; contraction of blood vessels in the stomach and intestines and increased heart beat so that more blood can reach the skeletal muscles responsible for action; release of glycogen from the liver gives more energy and perspiration reduces body heat and prevents disabling rise in body temperature. The parasympathetic system works in exactly the opposite way, to conserve resources of the body; e.g. lowering of rate of breathing; decreasing heartbeat, etc. Its functioning leads to quiet, pleasurable peaceful existence.

It will at once be recognised that reactions such as salivation and control of bladder are the concern of the autonomic system and that the emotional reactions of classical conditioning are mediated by this system. For example, when Albert and Peter were frightened the sympathetic system was active. When Peter was quietly enjoying his lunch the parasympathetic was operating. The meaning of *reciprocal inhibition* should now be clear. The effects of the sympathetic system are counteracted by that of the parasympathetic and in this way direct unconditioning, as employed by Miss Cover Jones, can take place. Peter was giving a sympathetic response to the rabbit; unconditioning depended on getting him to make a parasympathetic response to the creature.

FURTHER READING

Morgan, and King (80), Hilgard (52), and Sanford (96) are good psychology textbooks with which to supplement knowledge of classical conditioning. Eysenck (32) provides an interesting and readable account of the use of reciprocal inhibition in behaviour therapy. The student wishing to follow the suggestion made on page 53 should try Borger and Seaborne (13, chapter 4); and Miller (76, chapter 13), or Hebb (50, chapter 5). It will probably be wisest to postpone this reading until after studying the next chapter of this book.

5 Operant Conditioning and Basic Learning Processes

Examples of operant conditioning

Imagine a hungry rat, a favourite laboratory animal, in a cage containing a lever which, when pressed, delivers a pellet of food into a box at the side of the bar-press. The rat, having the tendencies (mentioned in chapter 3, p. 29) to explore and to act, runs around smelling here and poking there, touching this and that, including in due course the lever. He does not notice the dispensed food pellet at once, but later finds it and eats it. In future explorations he looks frequently at the box and after pressing the lever sees and eats another pellet. The next time the bar is pressed he sees the pellet quickly and eats it at once, and thereafter the number of bar pushes increases rapidly until he is working hard and fast at lever pressing by which he obtains a good supply of food. The rat has achieved instrumental or operant learning, that is, he has learned by producing his own *reinforcement* or reward.

I am just out of bed, slippers are on and dressing-gown is quickly taken from the left side of the wardrobe; downstairs I fill and plug in the electric kettle, collect the red tea tin from the larder and assemble cup, saucer and infuser from cupboard and drawer. Very soon, binoculars at my side, I am sitting, reinforced by tea and a view of early morning birds. Consider the same sequence on the first day at a hired holiday cottage. 'Where did I put my dressing-gown? How does this kettle plug in? Which of these tins contains tea? The cups must be in the other cupboard.' Eventually with the reinforcing brew in hand, 'Where shall I sit to get the best view of the morning-lit lough?' In the first case I ran through, 'without let or hindrance', a sequence of well-learned operant behaviour. In the second case I was learning operantly.

To study operant conditioning at its simplest, we will return to the rat. How has this new behaviour, regular lever pressing, come about? Some actions produced a reward, that is satisfied a need, in this case produced food to reduce hunger pangs. These actions, lever pressing, were repeated, while other actions which were not rewarded or reinforced dropped out. There are several ways of describing this process:

1. During successive trials correct or rewarded actions were repeated while unrewarded actions or errors were discontinued;
2. The rat's behaviour was instrumental in bringing about reward;
3. The rat operated to bring about a reward.

Historically, this type of learning has been known as trial-and-error learning (frequently associated with E. L. Thorndike (1874–1949)), instrumental learning and operant learning (very commonly associated with B. F. Skinner, a leading contemporary psychologist).

Like classical conditioning, operant conditioning can be shown diagrammatically. R1 R2 R3 .... Rx .... Rn represent an active creature's responses as it explores its environment, and Sr_s and Rr_s are stimuli and responses in the reinforcing event.

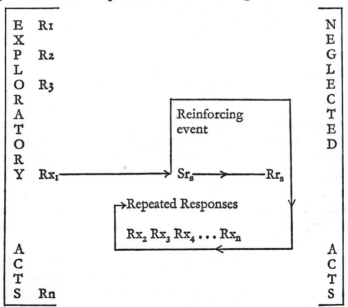

It is possible to say that an association has been made between Rx, e.g. bar pressing and the reinforcing experience, e.g. seeing and eating food, and that this association has increased the likelihood of the repetition of Rx_1, e.g. Rx_2, Rx_3, etc. In chapter 2 it was made clear that creatures behaved selectively to satisfy needs. The experiment described shows how an animal may learn to do this. A stimulus (the bar) at first is merely the object of the 'what-is-it?' reaction, but it comes by association with a satisfying event (seeing and eating food) to be itself a stimulus for satisfaction of an immediate need (hunger), and thus it will be selectively acted or operated upon. *Reinforcement* is thus well defined as an event (getting food) which increases the probability that a particular response or group of responses will be repeated. It is interesting to note that sometimes a creature will make an entirely superfluous act when producing reinforcement and this act will also tend to be repeated, e.g. as a result of accidentally scratching his head while pressing a lever, a monkey may afterwards always scratch while lever pressing. Skinner calls such acts, superstitious acts. As an example of the operant conditioning of an animal outside the laboratory we may take the now common occurrence of tits pecking holes in milk bottle tops to be rewarded by a creamy, or perhaps only homogenised, milk drink. In neither of the examples given was an attempt made to train the animals, but the fact that reinforcement leads to the repetition of acts has for centuries been used in animal training.

Shaping
Operant conditioning as a method of training animals, notably pigeons, has been extensively studied in the laboratory. Feeding is used as the reinforcement or 'consequence' of the acts which are to be conditioned. The process of conditioning is facilitated by a piece of preliminary training. If a pigeon is repeatedly presented with food from a dispenser which makes a sharp click as food is delivered, then he will, by classical conditioning, come to associate the click with feeding responses, e.g. looking for and at food, approaching tray, eating, etc. (Note the difference between these reactions and the reactions to food during classical conditioning when the animal is restrained, as in Pavlov's experiments.) The

click is now, by association, satisfying, and its presentation, like the presentation of food, will serve to increase the probability of an action which precedes it. Such reinforcement is known as *secondary reinforcement* and it is a great help in operant conditioning because it can instantly follow a response. Secondary reinforcement is especially useful as a means of shaping behaviour which is a particular form of operant conditioning. An amusing account of the first shaping to be done using a hand food dispenser is given by B. F. Skinner (97, page 132). The experimental pigeon had, as already described, fed repeatedly from the hand food-magazine and Skinner writes,

...in getting it (the piegon) to respond to the sound of the magazine by turning immediately and approaching the food tray – we had created an auditory *conditioned reinforcer*.

One day we decided to teach a pigeon to bowl. The pigeon was to send a wooden ball down a miniature alley toward a set of toy pins by swiping the ball with a sharp sideward movement of the beak. To condition the response, we put the ball on the floor of an experimental box and prepared to operate the food magazine as soon as the first swipe occurred. But nothing happened. We decided to reinforce any response which had the slightest resemblance to a swipe – perhaps, at first, merely the behaviour of looking at the ball – and then to select responses which more closely approximated the final form. The result amazed us. In a few minutes the ball was caroming off the walls of the box as if the pigeon had been a champion squash player.

How can this rapid learning be explained? The first piece of behaviour which would lead the animal towards the desired pattern of responses was immediately reinforced by the click and the probability of its repetition was thereby increased. When next made, if followed by another item of behaviour leading towards the target performance, then this move is also rewarded and the likelihood of the two moves occurring again and beginning to form the required pattern is heightened. Reinforcing in such a manner is known as *reinforcing a series of successive approximations* and it is a method of teaching which can be employed in some human learning situations as well as in animal training.

In the shaping of behaviour just described the reward or rein-forcement was extrinsic to the task (cf. chapter 2). Operant learning also functions in the development of skills where the reinforcement is intrinsic to the task and serves its function by giving information or feedback indicating success. To watch a baby beginning to walk or a toddler starting to throw a ball is to see behaviour *taking shape* as a result of differential reinforcement through FEEDBACK. In the first case, reinforcement comes from the feel of the activity; the feel of a move which is successful is the reinforcer which will lead to the probability of repetition; the feel of unsuccessful moves will not be reinforcing, because not accompanied by satisfaction. In the second case, the reinforcement will be due both to the feeling produced by successful moves and to visual stimuli such as noticing how far the ball goes, etc. Normally it is difficult to appreciate, at first hand, how such differential reinforcement works. Either one has acquired a skill, and it has become automatic and habitual, or one is concentrating on the task and cannot attend to anything but the actual making of moves. However, in certain unusual circumstances one may become aware of this shaping by feedback, e.g. getting one's sea legs on board ship or using the other hand when one's preferred hand is injured. In the former case it is perhaps when returning to land that one is most conscious of the corrective feedback as one re-adapts to normal walking. An understanding of reinforcing feedback is essential for formal training of any skill. The teacher or trainer must be responsible for setting standards of proximate goals and target behaviour and for giving knowledge of results which provide corrective feedback. Skilled behaviour can then be shaped. (N.B. It is possible for a learner to train himself; training does not necessarily imply a teacher.) But a teacher specifically undertakes to arrange circumstances so that the learner may receive, by one means or another, access to knowledge of results which then provide corrective feedback and reinforcement. An example may be given here to show how knowledge of results may *reinforce* in *shaping* discriminative behaviour by the method of *successive approximation*. Holland and Matthews (55) taught children who had difficulty in discriminating and articulating *s* sounds. The children had first to discriminate between *s* sounds and others and then to hear differences between different *s*s, as for, example, in *post* and *posy*. The method consisted of asking a child to listen to a tape recording and to press labelled buttons when certain sounds were heard. When the child pressed a correct button he was immediately rewarded by a flashing light giving knowledge of result and corrective feedback. The child was first presented with a particular *s* sound said louder than any others and repeated among other sounds very unlike any *s* sound. Next this sound was given at the same volume as the others. Then it was given with other sounds more similar to itself. Then several *s* sounds were given together and so on, until finally similar words were presented together, e.g. *ship* and *sip*. This method proved very successful and the children learned well to overcome a serious difficulty. Similar methods have been used to improve auditory discrimination in people previously thought to be tone deaf. In the normal school setting the use of such a method would be difficult, but some teaching machines and learning programmes are designed along these lines. Teachers, administrators and architects are becoming more aware of the need for very careful grading of work for individuals and groups and hence of the need for varying types of teaching equipment and space. Skinner has pointed out (97) that it may be dangerous to say that an individual cannot learn something for it may be that an effective work programme has not been arranged. The arrangement of an effective programme in the school situation may be complicated by the presence of motivation other than that related to the achievement brought about by corrective feedback and knowledge of results. In the last two chapters it was recognised that motivation could be very complex and a learner may no longer care whether he succeeds, or may already be conditioned to dislike school and so his emotion disrupts his work. Some of these practical problems will be considered later, and to round off this section on the shaping of behaviour we will quote another amusing passage from B. F. Skinner (97, page 418) showing the importance of shaping in social relationships. (It will be remembered from the last two chapters that human beings are socially motivated to receive attention and approval from others and that young children are especially dependent upon adults in this respect.)

... when she (mother) is busy, she is likely not to respond to a call or request made in a quiet tone of voice. The average intensity of the child's vocal behaviour therefore moves up to another level. . . . Eventually the mother gets used to this level and again reinforces only louder instances. This vicious circle brings about louder and louder behaviour. The child's voice may also vary in intonation, and any change in the direction of unpleasantness is more likely to get the attention of the mother and is therefore strengthened. . . . The mother behaves, in fact, as if she had been given the assignment of teaching the child to be annoying! The remedy is. . . .

But the reader may supply the remedy, and note that 'teacher' may be substituted for 'mother'.

REINFORCEMENT

It is obvious that reinforcement is a key factor in all operant learning. It has indeed been shown that work habits and extinction are very considerably affected by the way in which the operant learner is able to gain reinforcement. It is now necessary to consider the experimental study of this topic.

Reinforcement schedules

The experiments are usually carried out using hungry pigeons previously conditioned to feed from a clicking food dispenser. The birds normally 'work' in a well-ventilated, sound-proof box joined to another box which contains all the equipment necessary to regulate and record the course of the experiment. Fitted at the end adjoining the equipment box is a translucent disc beneath which is an aperture leading to the food tray. Shaping will quickly lead the pigeon to peck at the disc and it is now arranged that this pecking shall operate the food dispenser. Now we have the situation where the pigeon can be given pecking tasks which he will learn and perform because successful pecks can be rewarded, immediately by the click (secondary reinforcer) and afterwards by food (primary reinforcer). A recording device built into the equipment box keeps a cumulative record of all pecks made (see reading list, page 70). The simplest task which the bird can be given is that he shall peck at a lighted spot on the disc and this task has in fact been used to study SCHEDULES OF REINFORCEMENT. It was early found that for the pigeon to maintain pecking at the required spot it was not necessary to give him 100% reinforcement, i.e. it was not always necessary to reward every correct peck. (The automatic food dispenser could be set to give food for some and not for all pecks.) When only some correct pecks are rewarded reinforcement is said to be partial. There are two main kinds of partial reinforcement. The first is known as RATIO REINFORCEMENT and the second as INTERVAL REINFORCEMENT. Both ratio and interval reinforcement may be fixed or variable. Fixed ratio 10 (usually written (FR10)) means that reinforcement is given after every ten correct responses, while fixed interval 2 (FI2), means that reinforcement is given two minutes after the first response and at intervals of two minutes thereafter.

In the variable schedules reinforcement is given after an average number of responses or an average time. In (VR10) a response will be reinforced, on an average, after every 10 responses have been made, but sometimes four or five responses will produce a reward and at other times more than ten responses will need to be made before reinforcement. Similarly, for (VI2) reinforcement might be delivered after a few seconds and then not again for three or four minutes and so on. As would be expected the pigeons' 'work habits' reflect the schedule by which they are reinforced. A fixed ratio scale (cf. piece work) leads to highest rates of working. This would be expected, for the reinforcement is directly the result of the number of responses made. When using fixed ratio schedules it is possible after a period of training to speed up work by decreasing the actual reward. (Is this, perhaps why Trade Unions usually oppose piece-work rates?) A pigeon trained on FR10 can be moved to FR20 and later, even, to FR100 and he will work faster and faster to gain his accustomed reward. If the FR is put very high, however, the animal will tend to take long rests after each reinforcement and then work very fast; this may lead to strain and then the animal breaks down. A variable ratio (cf. gambling) scale gives a much more stable performance – there are no long waits after reinforcement and no straining bursts of speed to be followed by breakdown. A similar difference, although not so marked, is seen between fixed (cf. weekly wage) and variable interval schedules (cf. many social reinforcers). A variable interval scale leads to very steady performance, e.g. pigeons reinforced by VR5 have been known to work for 15 hours making two or three pecks per second and never pausing for longer than 20 seconds during the whole period. In general the shorter the time between intervals (actual or average) the faster the speed of work. It seems that variable schedules are more efficient than fixed ones in producing stable work habits and this holds when animals are working on complex discriminatory problems as well as when they are simply pecking for the purpose of testing work schedules. Experimental psychologists, notably C. B. Ferster and B. F. Skinner (33) have experimented with complex schedules made up of the four types in various combinations. Skinner has commented (97) that just as a pattern of behaviour may be shaped, so work habits can be shaped by using appropriate schedules of reinforcement and thus enabling a worker to use his full learning and working power.

It will be clear that evidence relating to human reinforcement is one very relevant factor which should be considered in connection with the current controversies concerning the relative merits of continuous assessment and examinations.

The use of different reinforcing schedules not only affects work habits but also rates of extinction. It will be remembered that in classical conditioning extinction was brought about by removal of UCS. In operant conditioning it is brought about by cutting off reinforcement. In general, learning produced by total reinforcement requires fewer unreinforced trials before extinction occurs than does learning produced by partial reinforcement; and fixed ratio scales lead to more easily extinguished behaviour than do variable scales. These facts may be explained by reference to generalisation of behaviour. The biggest difference between the learning and working situation and the extinction event occurs when there is a change from continuous, 100%, to zero reinforcement, and thus response generalisation will be at a minimum. At first, however, the extinction condition may seem little different from partial and variable schedules and response generalisation will be maximised. If the subjects were men, rather than pigeons, we should say that the worker, like the gambler, was hoping for a run of good luck or high reinforcement and so kept on working.

The advantage to educational psychology and educational practice of such detailed work with pigeons is that the basic principles pertaining to reinforcement can be detected, uncluttered by all the complicating factors which exist in any human learning situation. But to know these principles is only a beginning and there are two ways of linking such observations to educational practice. One way is for the educational psychologist or the research worker to take over where the pure psychologist leaves off and to try out similar simplified experiments with human learners in controlled conditions in an effort to minimise extraneous factors. For example, D.J. Lewis (65) had four groups of $6\frac{1}{2}$ to $7\frac{1}{2}$-year-old boys play a 'gambling' game, by operating a machine by which they could win or lose small toys, and each group were rewarded with toys on a different reinforcement schedule, namely continuous – 100%, 60%, 50% or zero rewards. The three reinforced groups underwent extinction trials and it was found that the partially reinforced groups were much more resistant to extinction than the continuously reinforced group. It will be recognised that these results confirmed expectations from the laboratory animal work. J. L. Bruning (20) conducted a rather similar experiment where $5\frac{1}{2}$- to $6\frac{1}{2}$-year-olds obtained sweets from a machine by operating a lever. Those reinforced on a 50% schedule worked faster than those on 100% reward, thus again confirming expectations.

The second way of using results from experimental psychology is for teachers and research workers to come together to test existing practices, to devise new methods of learning and teaching which use as many of the psychological findings as possible, and to try out these methods with adequate numbers and control groups (cf. Introduction). The need for evidence relating to student reinforcement has already been mentioned. A carefully recorded study of student work habits in relation to various test procedures, established and newly devised, would be an instance of this second type of research work.

Negative reinforcement and avoidance learning
Positive reinforcement, so far considered, depends upon presenting some reward which can give satisfaction. (It should be

E

remembered that reward includes corrective feedback by know-ledge of results.) Negative reinforcement, now to be considered, depends upon presenting an unpleasant stimulus, and satisfaction comes when the aversive stimulus is either escaped from or successfully avoided. In studying avoidance learning, there will be an opportunity to see classical and operant conditioning functioning together, something which is continually happening in everyday life.

Imagine a dog in a compartment divided in two by a fence about as high as the dog's shoulder. A buzzer is sounded, the dog's ears prick up and then, after 10 seconds, the dog receives a shock to his paws from an electric grill on the floor. The dog yelps, squirms and then after some random movements jumps over the fence, thus *escaping* the shock. Watch the dog again after, say, twelve trials. The buzzer sounds and the dog is over the fence in a couple of seconds, well before the buzzer has finished and the shock turned on. The dog has now learned to *avoid* the shock. This learning can be accounted for by a combination of classical and operant conditioning. Diagrams used as previously can clearly show the total learning.

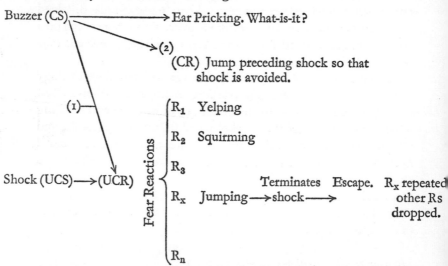

Buzzer (CS) ⟶ Ear Pricking. What-is-it?

(2)
(CR) Jump preceding shock so that shock is avoided.

(1)

Fear Reactions
{
R_1 Yelping

R_2 Squirming

R_3

R_x Jumping ⟶ shock ⟶   Terminates Escape. R_x repeated other Rs dropped.

R_n
}

Shock (UCS) ⟶ (UCR)

Once learned, such a response cannot be easily extinguished. The experimenter cannot follow the usual extinction procedure and cut off the UCS, i.e. shock, because the animal is no longer receiving any shock. After the initial learning a dog can be put into the compartment day after day and he will begin to jump as soon as the buzzer starts. By the same process if shock is given on both sides of the fence a dog will continue to jump back and forth (101). The lack of extinction is perhaps the most interesting and significant factor in this experiment for it provides the middle events to the story of the origin and cure of fears mentioned in the last chapter. It is now possible to appreciate how fears are maintained. Operant learning subsequent to the initial fright keeps the subject away from the contacts which could prove the fear groundless, and this is why a person like Peter in the last chapter may need help in overcoming an irrational fear (cf. 'further reading' for chapter 4).

Avoidance learning is motivated by 'punishment', i.e. by the application of an unpleasant stimulus. It has already been shown that it is effective in bringing about learning which leads to escape and avoidance, for the dog in the experiment learned when and where to jump. He did not need to learn *how* to jump for he already possessed that skill, but rats have been conditioned to fear a compartment from which they can then escape, and they have learned to operate quite complicated devices to open the door. Thus it is justifiable to say that punishment can lead to new skills when the learning brings escape or avoidance (77). But, normally, 'punishment' is not given with the intention that the culprit shall learn to get away. If a boy is punished for producing careless work in algebra it is not the intention of the teacher that the pupil shall carry out 'avoiding algebra actions' though in practice this may happen, either at once, or when the course is over, even if it is successfully completed. Punishment, in the colloquial (non-technical) sense of the word, is usually given with the intention of changing or extinguishing a bad habit. Is there evidence from experimental work that it can do this? Consider the following experiment. Two rats were each trained to press a bar in the usual way and then extinction trials began. Both rats received no further food reinforcement but in addition one rat received punishment, and on the first few trials he was rapped over the paws as he pressed the bar. His rate of responding was for a time lower than that of the unpunished rat, but very soon he began to press at a high rate and in the end the number of responses needed for extinction was approximately the same for punished and unpunished rats. The experiment was repeated with other pairs of rats but this time the punishment was much more severe. The punished rat was subjected to shock at every press. The extinction took place rapidly, but not only was this behaviour stopped, the whole of the rat's behaviour was disrupted and he broke down. Mild punishment appears on this evidence to be ineffective, and severe punishment disruptive, but it should be noticed that for the experimental animals there were no alternative actions available. We may look to ethology to see an example of animal punishment in a natural setting. Dr Jane van Lawick Goodall (41) has observed chimpanzee mothers caring for their children and has observed that they use the technique of distraction. Of a particular chimp preventing a four-year-old from touching a young baby she says, 'first she merely pushed the child's hand away. Then if this failed she groomed or played with Fifi until her attention was distracted from the baby – for a while anyway. And then the whole pattern of events was repeated.' A mild punishment which stops an activity long enough for another to be started may be effective if alternatives are readily available for new learning. A parent or teacher who says *no* firmly and then offers an alternative may be providing all the punishment that is necessary. The mother who says *no* and provides no alternative will probably do little to extinguish the undesirable behaviour. After her back is turned she is likely to complain, 'he's at it again', for she will have done nothing to provide new motivation so that the child can be selectively active in a new way; and, as we saw in chapter 2, a lively creature will usually be active in some way.

Comparison of classical conditioning CR–1 and operant conditioning CR–2

In chapter 3 the term *reinforcement* was not used, though some psychologists regard the UCS as the reinforcer. Undoubtedly in some cases of classical conditioning the UCS is a reinforcing stimulus, e.g. food is a positive reinforcer and shock a negative one. But is *being awakened by an alarm bell* properly called a reinforcer? There are those who argue that for the enuretic desiring cure it may be so. (One little girl, delighted to be cured, is reported to have said, 'Ting-a-ling is my best friend'.) There are other theorists who wish to give the term *reinforcement* a more restricted and specialised meaning than that given to the word *reward*, but this does not resolve the question as to whether pairing of UCS and CS is alone sufficient for learning to take place by means of classical conditioning. A final answer to this question will probably only be found when more is known about the functioning of the central nervous system in relation to pleasure. At present, fascinating investigations are being made in this direction which, as is not infrequently the case, began as a result of an accident. J. Olds and P. Milner (86) were studying the effects of direct stimulation of rats' brains. (This can be done painlessly after an operation by which a minute electrode is implanted in the brain.) One day, unexpectedly, they found that when a certain part of the brain was stimulated the stimulus acted as a reinforcer. They found, for example, that if this area of the brain was stimulated when the rat was in a certain place then he would return again and again to that place. He also learnt to run a maze when the reward at the end was such stimulation. In subsequent research it was arranged that the rats could stimulate themselves by pressing a lever as in the experiment already described. The rats would work for hours pressing levers to get stimulation just as they press them to be rewarded by food. It was found by this research that only a very circumscribed part of the brain reacts to stimulation in this way. Further investigations of this problem may lead to greater understanding of the learning processes.

In the last chapter extinction, generalisation and discrimination were considered as basic learning processes; they have been referred to in this chapter and it must be pointed out that they are equally important in both types of conditioning. Further, a reminder must be given that a high proportion of responses learned by the method of classical conditioning are controlled by the autonomic nervous system and that this is not so for operant conditioning.

CONCLUSION

Minimum information required for habituation to take place is derived from the repetition of a single stimulus, while classical conditioning requires information from the repetition of at least two stimuli. Operant conditioning depends upon the selection of responses. After selection, the relevant information is 'this response rewards' but the amount of information required for selection is variable. The selection may be independent of information leading to superstitious acts; it may result from calculated risk taking or from the accumulated knowledge and wisdom of a lifetime. Where in this hierarchy lies the flash of genius that leads to an act of originality or creativity? This is a problem of great and recurrent interest.

SUMMARY

Operant conditioning depends on reinforcement which increases the probability that an act will be repeated. Shaping leads to learning through the method of reinforcing a series of successive approximations. Reinforcement may be positive or negative and may be either extrinsic reward, or knowledge of results. Schedules of reinforcement influence both work habits and speed of extinction.

FURTHER READING

Skinner (97). This is a collection of articles showing the author's work connected with operant conditioning and its applications. There is much in it that should prove interesting especially in parts III and VIII. In part III will be found an explanation of the term *cumulative record*. A novel, Skinner (98) may prove interesting and thought provoking.

Miller (76, chapters 13 and 14) and Foss (35, chapters 15 and 16) will supplement many points made in this chapter. Important links between this chapter and chapters 2 and 3 can be seen by reading Argyle (3, chapter 10).

Readings connected with this chapter will be found in De Cecco (27).

Interested students should read further about programmed learning; many books are available and Apter (2) introduces this topic and gives a full bibliography.

6 Remembering and Forgetting

Perceptual learning

One form of perceptual learning is that which alters the manner of our future perceptions. One example of this type of perceptual learning was mentioned in connection with the effects of early experience (page 18). Continued practice improves a Western child's ability to distinguish one European face from another, while lack of similar perceptual learning with regard to Oriental faces makes distinction between them difficult. Sometimes, such perceptual learning can be a hindrance because it may make it difficult to see the environment in a new way, and it is often important to do this when an unusual problem has to be solved. We shall return to this, the topic of perceptual rigidity, in the next chapter when dealing with problem solving.

There is another, and perhaps simpler, form of perceptual learning. To consider it, let us return to the holiday cottage where I made early morning tea. Now, later on the first day, I am preparing picnic sandwiches. 'Ah yes, there is a cheese grater underneath the shelf where I found the tea tin.' And in answer to the question, 'Is there a screwdriver here?' 'Well, there are some tools under the stairs, behind the brushes.' I have evidently learned, in passing, a number of things about this cottage. I have gathered up some knowledge which can be used when required, but at the time of gaining it I made no response. Thus such learning must be the result of association between stimuli, that is S→S connections have been made.

It may now be asked how much background knowledge for future use can be acquired by S→S learning. Some psychologists would suggest that as a housewife I would notice and remember only what would be useful in carrying out housewifely activities.

But I am not interested in tools, although I had noted their whereabouts. Other psychologists would suggest, and it is the suggestion already made in this book, that such learning is the human equivalent of the learning done by the animals as they explore. As such, the learning satisfies a general drive and needs no further special explanation in terms of particular motives. (For experimental evidence relating to the establishment of this position see reading list, page 94.) it is, however, not denied that when many stimuli and little time are available (a state too common with many of us), then we shall chiefly notice and store knowledge of the things for which our past experience has prepared us and to which present activities direct us (see ATTENTION. page 131). Knowledge gained will then be available for further use. There is, however, an important point to be made with regard to the retention of the knowledge gained by perceptual learning. Writing now, at home, and nearly twelve months after the holiday, I can still remember the position in that cottage kitchen of the things which I used and from the use of which I gained reinforcement. But there were many things which I did not use and I cannot now recall where they were kept, though at the time, had I needed them, I should have known where they were to be found. Operant learning, subsequent to perceptual learning, has increased the length of the memories. But I remember, too, the position of the screwdriver and this I did not use. This item of perceptual knowledge, alone of the unused items, has been retained. Could this be because I had actively recognised and noted the relationship between the position of the tools and the operantly learned position of the brushes? The tools I stated were *behind* the brushes and thus I expressed a relationship which I had observed because of previously well learned spatial concepts. Earlier evidence of operant learning allows us to accept the supposition that perceptual knowledge will be retained as a result of reinforced operant learning. The second suggestion, that actively perceiving relationships increases retention, needs further investigation. It was mentioned in chapter 1 and it is, of course, well recognised that much of human knowledge is derived from symbols so it will be well to make our investigation of active memorisation in relation to such material. In studying memorisation it will be necessary to study the two related processes of remembering, namely recognition and recall.

MEMORISING AND REMEMBERING

Useful knowledge

An examination of a simple experiment will best serve to introduce memorisation of new symbolic material and draw attention to features of memorising which lead, later, to the ready use of that material, i.e. lead to useful knowledge. I. M. L. Hunter (59, page 22) reports that he has given the following task of learning and recall to over 200 students. I have given it to some thirty students. The responses of my students were substantially the same as those reported by Hunter and I shall here report, in full, the comments of five students which are representative. It is relevant to do this as these individual comments will clearly make an important point in relation to memorisation, namely, that methods of memorising and recalling are to some extent idiosyncratic.

$$4 \quad 9 \quad 2$$

$$3 \quad 5 \quad 7$$

$$8 \quad 1 \quad 6$$

Students were told that for one minute they would be allowed to look at an array of numbers. (The one shown above.) They were asked to work hard throughout the minute so that they would learn and be able to reproduce the array. At the end of the lecture time, about fifty minutes later, they were asked to make their reproduction and to write down how they had set about learning and recalling the task. The following are the comments made by the five representative students.

A. I noticed that the left-right diagonal had 4, 5 and 6 along it, which was easy, and I saw that the middle row had odd numbers 3, 5, and 7 which was also easy. I then saw that the top spaces were filled with 9 and 2 and the bottom with 8 and 1. 9^2 is 81 so this too was easy. (She had indeed a system here by which, later, she was able to reproduce the whole.)

B. I looked for something which I knew. Telephone numbers or house numbers. No luck. I then saw 492 and remembered 'In 1492 Columbus sailed the ocean blue'. This gave me the top line, but I could find nothing else so I began to recite 357 and 816 over and over again.

C. 27th of June is my birthday, this gave me the last column. I saw that a diagonal was 4, 5 and 6 and then that all the rows made 15, so I was O.K. (In fact she wasn't – she got the 8 and the 1 the wrong way round. She needed to know that columns as well as rows totalled 15.)

D. I saw that every line added to 15, and that even numbers were at the corners with the smallest at the top and the right. (She had enough information here to fill up the square systematically and get it right.)

E. I tried saying 492, 357, 816 over and then 438, 951, 276, but when I came to recall I got in an awful muddle.
(This student was the only one who made more than two errors. It is interesting to note that she was, also, the only one who was uneconomical in repetition, that is, she repeated numbers in two ways where one way would have been sufficient.)

It is at once clear that each student devised some method or scheme for memorising and it is interesting and important to appreciate that, with the exception of E, who experienced difficulty in reproduction, no student commented on the activity of recall. Evidently, all thought it obvious that the system for recall would be the same as that for memorising. This assumption, based on common experience, is worthy of attention for it suggests that failure to recall may be partially due to unsystematic or disorganised learning and not always to the passage of time as is popularly supposed. The suggestion that organisation for recall is important must be pursued further and, as a beginning, it will be profitable to list the strategies for memorising shown by these students. There was:

(a) effort to make a link between the new material and past personal experience, e.g. birth date, house number;

(b) a search for connections with past learning, e.g. Columbus-1492, $9^2 = 81$;

(c) formation and naming of groups, e.g. even numbers are corner numbers, and of sub-groups, e.g. smallest even numbers are at top and right;

(*d*) noting of sequences, e.g. along the middle row and the left-right diagonal;

(*e*) formation of rules, e.g. all rows, columns and diagonals total 15.

These strategies for memorising appear to be devices for connecting past experience and learning with new material. An idiosyncratic link may be discovered as in (*a*). General information such as $9^2 = 81$ may be used in an unexpected context, so forming a somewhat unusual connection as in (*b*). Connections may, as in (*c-e*), lead to classification and rule making based on commonly held concepts, and such connections will be impersonal and widely used. For example, the connections used in learning the number array are those based on familiar concepts of a universally established number system.

Hunter reports that there were very few students who learnt by mere repetition, that is by repeating the numbers without noticing relationships between them. If rote learning is uncommon in memorising a simple task which can be mastered by approximately 90% of learners in one minute, then it is surely likely to be even less used when larger amounts of more complex material are studied over longer periods of time. It may well be asked why this is so and the query may best be dealt with by considering difficulties of recall which are usually felt as a result of sheer rote learning. For example, when I was a child I learnt by rote the jingle which begins:

> Willie, Willie, Harry, Ste,
> Harry, Dick, John, Harry three. . . .

The rhyme is useful if I wish, now, to remember the order of English monarchs, but if I am asked a question such as 'who followed Richard II?' I cannot immediately say 'Henry IV', and I do not feel certainly correct if I say to myself only the couplet:

> One, two, three Neds, Richard II
> Harrys four, five, six, then who?

To be sure of my answer I have to recite from line one up to the occurrence of the required name.

Now, clearly, this is an uneconomical method of recall and yet it is the only consistently safe method if the memorising has been by mechanical rote learning. In earlier days of less enlightened teaching of arithmetic it was not uncommon to find children who could only perform the operation of, say, 9×9 by reciting the table from 9×1 up to the appropriate point. The disadvantage of rote learning is not confined to 'by heart' memorising. If material is learned by repetitive follow-through, with no attempt at organisation, then it will be difficult to recall component items out of their original context, and such learning will not provide knowledge which is readily available in a variety of circumstances. When a task is both easy and short, such as learning the number array, repetitive learning may result in successful recall; however, it will be unsatisfactory for any but the most simple task just because it does not lead to economical ways of recall but only to recall by laborious repetition.

It is now possible to see more clearly how memorising strategies bring about efficient ways of recall. The strategies may be compared to methods of constructing an adequate filing system. By the analogy, items are thought of as being filed in various ways. Some new items will be filed with previously stored knowledge, some as examples of known classes and relationships, and still others as exemplifying a rule based upon a well-known principle. On the occasion of recall it is these connections, classes, relationships and rules which are retrieved and reconstruction of the material then follows. Thus recall is not merely retrieval from store but an *active process of reconstruction*.

The unfortunate children who were made to learn 'tables' before experience and perception of number relationships could not employ the strategies for memorising, so that learning and recall were both tied to unorganised rote repetition. After meaningful number experiences, of the kind now commonly provided, children can memorise by connecting symbolic expressions with known relationships, and recall will be possible in a variety of ways, as, for example, in the number games and drills of the primary school which lead towards the solution of problems by the readily available knowledge of number products.

Organised, or strategic, memorising leads to *economical recall* and to the ready availability of knowledge, because the recall of a *single* relationship or rule may generate several items for the process of reconstruction. Moreover, wise choice of rule or relationship can maximise the number of items gained by the recall of a single principle. For example, a very efficient way of learning the number array is to observe (1) the position of the sequence 3, 4, 5 and (2) *the rule* that all lines (columns, rows and diagonals) total 15. Thus the learner is dealing in recall with only two principles and not with nine items as in rote learning or with three or four relationships and rules when other sequences are chosen. This principle of economy used in building an individual memory store continues to be important in building the bodies of knowledge which represent men's cumulative study. The elegance of economy is sought in linguistic exposition, mathematical proof, scientific rigour and artistic design. Thus it is that the symbolic material which we need to memorise is readily susceptible to our strategies. Is it possible for psychologists to investigate further, and perhaps further explain or account for this important principle of economy?

As early as 1859 Sir William Hamilton, a Scottish philosopher, told his students that if they threw a handful of marbles on the floor, they would 'find it difficult to view at once more than six, or seven at most, without confusion; but if you group them into twos, or threes or fives, you can comprehend as many groups as you can units because the mind considers these groups only as units' (43 and 117). In 1871 W. S. Jevons, a logician and economist, made an extremely thorough study of his own SPAN OF APPREHENSION. His method was to place a white tray on a larger black one, throw black beans on to the white tray, and after each throw make an immediate estimate of how many beans were on the white tray. The following table shows what percentage of his estimates were correct (117, page 91)

Actual no. of beans	3	4	5	6	7	8	9	10	11	12	13	14	15
% of correct estimates	100	100	95	82	75	56	62	43	38	42	23	29	18

It will be seen that when the number was more than 9, Jevons's estimate was more likely to be wrong than right. When the number was five or less he would certainly, or very probably, under more controlled conditions and using a variety of stimuli make a correct judgement. Subsequent experiments performed have confirmed that the pattern of Jevons's results is typical of the performance of most adults, though the rate of fall off in accuracy will to some extent vary with individual differences in general ability. Such experiments suggest that normally 7 ± 2 is the number of items which can be attended to or 'held' at once. Similar results are given for memory span. Studies of immediate memory have shown, through carefully controlled experiments, that a normal adult who listens to a random series of digits, letters or monosyllables can usually correctly repeat a sequence of no more than 5–9 items. Note, however, that in repeating 5–9 monosyllables he is in fact remembering some 20–30 letters. Similarly 5–9 meaningful words containing perhaps some 20 syllables can be repeated; and a group of perhaps 3 short sentences can be remembered, for though they may be made up of more than 5–9 words they may contain only 5–9 phrases or ideas. Our immediate or 'holding' memory span is obviously improved if we are recalling informationally rich or meaningful symbols rather than limited ones. G. A. Miller has said (76, page 4), 'Obviously we will carry more wealth if we fill the purse with silver dollars rather than with pennies'. (The study of the amount of information carried by various symbols and symbolic expressions is being carried out by means of the mathematical theory of communication.) (See reading list, page 94.)

It is clear that here is the explanation for both the economy of symbolic expression and for the widespread use of memorising strategies. Bodies of knowledge will be expressed in richly meaningful symbols and these will aid the learner when he is selecting strategies to suit his own past experience and learning. The amount of *readily available or useful knowledge* will depend upon the inclusiveness of this 'filing system' which has been designed to minimise the 'holding' during the process of constructive recall. J. S. Bruner has said, 'compacting or condensing is the means whereby we fill our seven slots with gold rather than dross' (18, page 12).

Cognitive development and memorising

Any student who has read one of the many available 'guides to study' will have recognised that the advice given is based upon the principles of memorising which have just been outlined. Though different guides may vary in detail, in general they offer the same advice:

1. Skim through section (usually a chapter).
2. Do not read passively. Read actively, that is, seek answers to your own questions aimed at linking the new material with your past experience and learning.
3. Organise the material for storage, by arranging under headings which are appropriate for you (note-making).
4. Test your own storage system by constructively recalling without books and notes.
5. Check.
6. Revise frequently, gradually lengthening the intervals between revision.

Consider the above in relation to your reading of the first part of this chapter.

Suitable questions under (2) above are:

(a) Have I ever experienced difficulties because of previous perceptual learning?
(b) How do I set about recalling a learned task?
(c) Do I possess any purely rote information? Is it useful? How and why did I acquire it?
(d) Have I noticed that children differ in any way because of different perceptual learning at an earlier stage? etc. etc.

What is the purpose of such active questioning by the reader? The purpose is to ensure that the new ideas are meaningful to the reader because linked with his past experience.

The next questions are designed in order to find connections between new material and earlier learning in relation to the same topic, and answers to the questions will aid organisation for storage.

(e) What references are there to the perceptual learning of children considered in chapter 2, page 18, and why is the reference made?

(f) What is the link between motivation as mentioned in this chapter and as mentioned earlier?

(g) What is the motivation for rote learning?

(h) What associations are made in rote learning?

(i) Is there reinforcement in this kind of memorisation; if so, what is it?

(j) Can this form of learning be subsumed under the heading of operant learning; if so how?

The last two of the above questions will have made apparent the need for the first instruction, namely, the instruction to skim through a chapter. If this has been done, then the reader will know that these questions will be dealt with, and, later, on reaching this part of the chapter he will be alert and ready to read purposefully.

Having seen connections between this material and other material of the same kind, the reader is now ready to continue with organisation as in (3) above by deciding upon suitable headings for arranging the new ideas. This might lead to such questions as:

(k) Do I understand the 'filing' metaphor?

(l) What points must be listed under 'constructive recall'?

The more thorough the organisation now, the more likelihood of correct recall, but 4, 5 and 6 follow to consolidate the learning and prevent forgetting. The effectiveness of these processes in relation to forgetting will be considered later.

It is assumed that after stimulus from teachers, students, and at least fifth- and sixth-formers, can manage their own learning along the lines suggested, and it is supposed that they have the necessary linguistic skills to interpret new concepts in terms of their past experience. From preliminary studies of the development of children most readers are likely to know that these assumptions are not justified for younger learners. The reader may not yet have made a detailed study of children's cognitive development exemplified by the work of J. Piaget in Geneva and J. Bruner at Harvard, and such a study is beyond the scope of this book. It should, however, be noted that in early years organised symbolic memorisation is not only inappropriate but also impossible. By their activities, children very gradually gain the basic concepts of space (beneath, left, - - -), time (soon after - - -), measurement, etc, and all the familiar concepts shared by members of the culture. These concepts are symbolised in the language which the children must simultaneously acquire, and as was seen in the case of memorising 'tables', effective learning can only take place if the language or other symbolism can be representative of concepts rooted in experience. Concepts and language are only gradually acquired, but the description of memorisation given here highlights the unity of the total learning process. Active memorisation as distinct from mechanical rote learning cannot take place without understanding but as concepts are acquired, language and symbols learned, so memorising becomes possible and a store of knowledge is gradually made. J. S. Bruner has listed some 'benchmarks' of intellectual growth. The second is, 'Growth depends upon internalising events into a "storage system" that corresponds to the environment', and the fourth is 'Intellectual development depends upon a systematic and contingent interaction between a tutor and a learner' (18, pages 5–6). These two principles, taken together, put meaning into educational slogans which are so often used without understanding. Activity learning, discovery learning, learning through experience, etc., are shorthand ways of saying that teachers must:

1. provide conditions in which new experiences may be gained;
2. encourage and direct translation of these experiences into the appropriate symbolic expression, at first spoken and later written;
3. afford opportunities and guidance for children to formulate questions, make discoveries and so connect past and present experiences (these activities are the equivalent of the student's self-questioning which is a necessary part of memorising);

F

4. enable children to extend their own first-hand experiences by listening to, watching and reading about the experiences of others, and so gradually acquire the concepts of their culture;

5. help children toward structuring their knowledge through varied forms of recording, both spoken and written, and through consulting references and texts (equivalent of students' note-making for organised storage);

6. arrange occasions for recall: number games have already been mentioned and there are countless forms of spoken and written work, tests, etc., etc. (cf. students' self-testing). Such activities must be varied to avoid boredom;

7. evaluate, correct, mark, etc. (cf. students' self-checking);

8. arrange for frequent revising, gradually lengthening intervals.

The emphasis placed on any one of these activities will, of course, vary with the age of the learners. (1) and (2) while always essential are almost exclusively so in a reception class. At the top of a primary school all are equally important and continue to be so, for all contribute to building a store of readily available knowledge.

When the above conditions for learning are fulfilled, children do not meet meaningless tasks of memorisation; but should they be unfortunate enough to do so then they will, as I. M. L. Hunter has pointed out, make an 'effort after meaning'. So-called 'howlers' occur when a child is valiantly trying to make sense of what to him is meaningless. It may be senseless to him either because he has not the necessary experience to understand the concepts symbolised, or because lack of linguistic skill has led him incorrectly to attach a familiar concept to an unfamiliar word. Fortunately, today, most teachers are sufficiently skilled to avoid situations such as this, but sometimes, thinking that they have given adequate opportunities for children to understand, teachers are surprised and disappointed when unexpected errors occur in recall. Frequently these may be attributed to a faulty link made by a child between his new learning and some prior personal experience. It will be when connecting new material with memories of past learning that the 'filing system' will become idiosyncratic (cf. page 75). While such individual links may be profitable, they may sometimes lead to incorrect linkages. The more personal the memory the more likely is it to lead to a howler. Having provided a laugh in the staff room such howlers should lead to careful restructuring of the child's perceived relationships. Such errors should make teachers aware that going over the original explanation will not necessarily help a child to correct a false insight gained by making a faulty connection between a new material and past experience. The secret of corrective teaching is for the teacher to understand why *this* learner made *this* mistake.

Uncategorised memory

It has probably already occurred to some readers that not all their memories result from processing material by acts of categorisation. It is indubitably the case that we can, perhaps by some single sensation such as smell, be reminded of a past experience and recall it with great clarity, often by way of IMAGERY. At such times we may recapture the details and the total *feel* of a particular event that we have certainly made no active effort to remember. Anyone who has experienced such nostalgic recollections will know at first hand that they bear little resemblance to the work-a-day memories carefully stored and recalled to provide answers to our practical and academic questions. There is also more objective evidence that memory storage exceeds that carried out by systematic effort. An eminent neurologist and brain surgeon, Wilder Penfield (89), during brain surgery, has observed the effect of a weak electrical stimulus applied to the surface of the patient's brain. When certain areas are stimulated the patient remembers events in such vivid detail that he seems to see again the total situation, to hear again the voices of those present, and to experience once more the emotions which he felt at the remembered time. Similarly, vivid recall can sometimes be effected by rhythmic stimulation of the eye with an intense and fast flickering light. W. Grey Walter reports that some patients, in states of mental strain, have responded to such stimulation... 'with a memory "as clear as crystal and as bitter as gall"...' (111, page 164). Apart from these clinical cases we each recognise as important our images of personal memory. These vivid memories enable us to appreciate and share analogous images which inspire poetry, literature and art, and we may vicariously experience the special and significant events which an artist describes. To foster such vivid memorisation is to preserve a child's sense of wonder and no teacher will wish to ignore this type of memory.

Forgetting

Lost without trace! So we may think as we struggle in vain for a name, a tune, a recipe, or the details of X's theory of Y. To a colleague, A says, 'I can't recall the name of that visiting lecturer who . . ., and yet I mentioned him last week.' 'Oh, yes, I remember him. Was his name Holbeach?' 'No, I'm sure it wasn't'. 'Holbeton or Holford?' 'No.' 'Holkham?' 'Yes that was it.' The name is not lost for it can be recognised. B unexpectedly finds himself humming the tune which earlier he could not recall and which he said he had forgotten. Father, shamefacedly, admits that he has forgotten when son seeks help in solving once familiar mathematical problems; mother cannot recall which is the appropriate bandage for a dislocated collar-bone. Those first-aid classes were a long time ago! But Dad takes the book and after a few minutes, 'Of course, I remember,' he says, and soon the problems are solved. Mother looks at several bandages, consults a diagram or two, and then, more deft than any beginner, fixes the sling. Clearly, to study forgetting is not an easy matter. If a tune can be forgotten at one time and recalled at another; if a name can be recalled at one time but only recognised at another; if Mum and Dad can quickly relearn, without repeating the initial process of organisation; then it follows that ability to recall is affected by factors over and above the effective organisation for storage so far considered. A common-sense suggestion was earlier noted (page 74), namely that although some forgetting depends upon degree of organised memorisation it is also in part due to the passage of time or to the course of events which fills that time.

Hermann Ebbinghaus (29) made the first, now classical, experimental studies of human memory. Of all his experiments, reported in 1885, the ones most often cited are those dealing with the process of forgetting in relation to the lapse of time. Ebbinghaus realised that in order to separate the effects of time from those of qualitative learning he must stabilise the learning pattern and measure precisely what had been learned and what, after an interval, could be recalled. For this purpose he devised nonsense syllables which are permanently linked with his name. He argued that lists of meaningless syllables like DAQ, XAJ, etc., would provide no associations and so no possibility of organisational learning, and thus he reasoned that all deterioration of ability to recall would be due to time factors and none due to the defects of organisation so far considered. Moreover, such material made it easy to specify exactly criteria of learning, e.g. a list may be counted as learned when it has been successfully repeated once, twice or n times; and equally easy to determine amount of recall, e.g. one, two, three or x items from the list. Ebbinghaus was his own subject and his procedure was to learn a group of eight lists of thirteen syllables until he had repeated each list twice through without error. He then recorded his learning time. After a specified interval he would endeavour to repeat the lists, and then record the time which he took to relearn them to the given standdard, e.g. twice through without mistake. Of course each group of lists could only be used once, but many such groups were learned, tested and relearned after different time intervals. After each attempt at recall and period of relearning, a calculation of the following kind was made.

$$\frac{\text{Original learning time } \textit{minus} \text{ relearning time}}{\text{Original learning time}} \times 100$$

Thus if 1010 secs were required for the original learning of eight lists, and if relearning time after 31 days was 803 secs, then the percentage saving would be calculated as $\frac{207}{1010} \times \frac{100}{1} = 20 \cdot 5\%$. This time, expressed as a percentage, is the time required to make knowledge originally retained again available. Such results are frequently shown graphically and the curves are traditionally known as retention curves which show the course of forgetting. Ebbinghaus's retention curve as presented by E. R. Hilgard (52, page 292) is given.

Curve of retention for lists of nonsense syllables (after Ebbinghaus 1885)

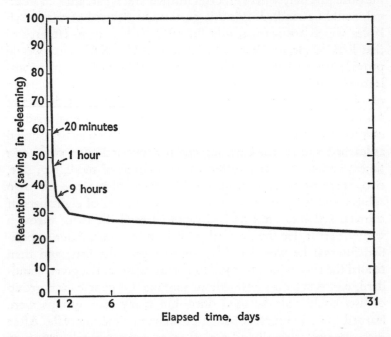

Ever since Ebbinghaus devised them, nonsense syllables have been used to study various problems of memorisation. The methods of presentation of the syllables have however been considerably improved. The syllables are frequently presented one at a time on a revolving drum, or on a screen, and after the first presentation of a complete list the subject learns by anticipating the next syllable. The process continues until the required standard is reached. Alternatively a list may be arranged and presented in the following way.

QEW
QEW – ZAJ

KEZ
KEZ – FUH etc.

After the first showing the learner, on seeing QEW, anticipates

ZAJ and then has his attempt corrected or confirmed by the presentation of QEW – ZAJ.

Here, our interest in these methods extends only to their use in relation to the study of forgetting. Using them, experiments similar to Ebbinghaus's original one have been repeated with many subjects and his results confirmed. Additional methods of calculating percentage measures of retention have been devised. The number of syllables recalled or recognised after a given interval are calculated as a percentage of the total list. A comparison of curves derived from the different measures shows that no matter what the measure, there is always a decrease in retention after a time lapse. The comparison also makes it very clear that relearning time is a sensitive measure showing that earlier learning may still be partially effective even when there is no evidence from recall or recognition.

Three measures of retention (after Luh 1922) Presented by E. R. Hilgard (52, page 293)

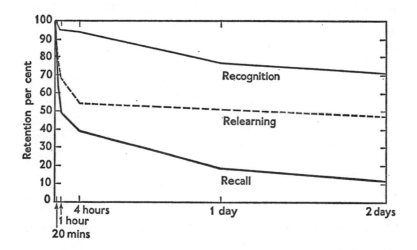

Under some conditions similarly shaped retention curves showing the course of forgetting have been gained by testing recall for meaningful material (see reading list, page 94.). However there were various observations which made for doubt as to whether the results were due simply to the passage of time. Ebbinghaus himself found some unexplained discrepancies in his results; for example, he noted that on one or two occasions increasing the interval between learning and recall by 60% produced an increase of 300% in the amount forgotten, which, compared with most of his results, was excessive. It was nearly thirty years before a satisfactory explanation was accepted for these discrepancies. It was then recognised that forgetting goes on at a slower rate during sleep than it does during waking hours. The first acceptable evidence was provided by J. G. Jenkins and K. M. Dallenbach in 1924 (62). The evidence resulted from a continuous record kept of the learning and recall of nonsense syllables by two subjects for a period of two months. Using an exposure apparatus, lists of 10 syllables were presented and the subject learned until he had successfully repeated the list once. During every day and night during the period of the experiment, lists were learned and recalled after 1, 2, 3, 4, or 8 hour periods of either sleeping or waking. Throughout the experiment the subjects and experimenter slept in a room adjoining the laboratory. The table below gives the average % recalled under the differing conditions (117, page 768).

		Intervals		
	1 hr	2 hrs	4 hrs	8 hrs
Awake	46	31	22	9
Asleep	70	54	55	56

This experiment was important because it led to intensive study of the effects of activities, preceding or following learning, upon ability to recall. Using nonsense syllable techniques many, many experiments have been carried out in order to gain knowledge about proactive (before learning) and retroactive (after learning) interference, which causes forgetting.

Proactive interference or inhibition

One experiment reported by B. J. Underwood (109) will serve to explain this cause of forgetting.

A group of subjects were each given a list of nonsense syllables to learn to a criterion of one perfect repetition. 24 hours later they repeated the list. It was found that the average correct recall was 80% of the items. 20% had been forgotten. Following the same procedures the subjects then learned and recalled another 19 lists on successive days. The average recall for the fourth list was 60%. 40% of the syllables had been forgotten. By the time the last list was recalled the average recall was only 20% and 80% of the list was forgotten. It is clear that the learning of the earlier lists has interfered with the recall of later lists, for normal sleeping and activity during 24 hours accounts for only 20% of forgetting. The reason for this interference is not difficult to find in terms of operant conditioning and though a little oversimplified may be given as follows. Whenever a list is learned, syllables which are correct for it are reinforced by corrective feedback and they will therefore be likely to be repeated (page 66). Thus whenever a new list is recalled some reinforced responses from past lists are likely to recur and form the mistakes of the new list.

Retroactive interference or inhibition

To measure retroactive interference it is necessary to have a control group and an experimental group (see Introduction). Both groups learn a list of nonsense syllables, list A, and then the experimental group learns another list of syllables, list B. Both groups are then tested for recall of list A and the difference between the recall scores of the control and experimental groups is a measure of the forgetting due to interference from list B. In one experiment carried out by A. W. Melton and J. Irwin (74) and (28) a number of such comparisons were made when different experimental groups repeated list B a variable number of times. It was found that when list B was repeated few times, items from that list intruded into list A and failure in accurate recall of list A was due both to these intrusions and to omissions. As repetitions of list B were increased, so intrusions from it into list A decreased, but omissions from A continued. These facts have been explained as follows. Repetition of list B leads to the reinforcement of its syllables and so increases the likelihood of their repetition, and thus they intrude into list A when it is recalled. As repetitions of list B increase it becomes much better learned and its syllables form a continuous sequence and are less likely to appear as isolates in list A. However, while list B is being repeated some items from list A will by proactive interference, intrude into it and these will never be reinforced. Thus they will be unlikely to be repeated when list A is recalled, and retroactive inhibition is causing the *unlearning* of list A by extinction. It has earlier been noted that passage of time leads to partial revival of extinguished responses (page 47) and this is the case here. Lengthening the time interval between the repetition of list B and testing list A leads to some improvement in the recall of list A.

Some recent studies, reported by J. Deese and S. H. Hulse (28) have been designed to test the effects of pro- and retro-active inhibition upon the retention of meaningful material. By using carefully designed experiments and very accurate measures of recall, evidence has been produced which suggests that effects of inhibition on curves of retention for meaningless and meaningful materials are similar in kind. L. Postman reviewing the evidence asks, 'Does interference theory predict too much forgetting?' (28, page 412) and suggests that the effect of inhibition on forgetting of meaningful material is lessened in proportion to the degree of organisation of the material during memorisation.

Operant learning has provided an explanation for inhibitory effects on forgetting nonsense material, and a tentative hypothesis may be put forward to explain its lessened effect upon forgetting meaningful material. Recall following upon organised memorisation is a constructive process. What is recalled is a minimum of items leading to reconstruction, and these items are frequently well learned and previously much reinforced relationships, rules, classes, concepts etc., etc. Such items of recall are not very likely to be unlearned by a process of extinction when another learning activity is in progress, and the existence of this holding framework is likely therefore to lessen the effects of inhibition.

It is now possible to account for the importance of revision which was mentioned earlier in this chapter, and which is usually stressed to both students and teachers. Until material is well organised for recall its component parts will be liable to interference from past and future learning activities. Frequent active revision in the early stages of learning will consolidate the organisation and so decrease the loss of separate items. Student teachers will perhaps recognise here the justification for planning lessons and work periods to allow both for revision of past work, which must, of course, be done in varied and interesting ways, and consolidation of present learning. They will perhaps also recognise the ill effects of rushing from one forty minute lesson or lecture to another without time for even preliminary organisation of new ideas. Primary schools frequently have flexible timetables but, at all levels of education, enquiries carried out by educational research workers and teachers in co-operation, are badly needed to find out more about forgetting in normal school circumstances and about arranging timetables for maximising learning efficiency.

Emotional factors in forgetting

The topic of forgetting cannot be left without reference to the emotional factors which are sometimes responsible for failure or mistaken recall. The study of such factors, frequently known as dynamic factors, derives from attempts to answer such questions as: Why do we more often forget the telephone number of our dentists than of our boy/girl friends? Why, when two honest and equally observant and systematic people report on the same event are there so frequently differences in testimony? The study of these factors, though important, is too complex for treatment here and the interested student should consult the reading list on page 94.

CONCLUSION

Strategies for organised memorising lead to quicker learning and slower forgetting than unorganised follow-through memorisation. Earlier, when thinking about motivation, a parallel was drawn between the active exploration of the environment and similar exploration of ideas by means of thought. To pursue this simile we may think of the organisation of new ideas, as considered in this chapter, as the charting or map-making of such intellectual exploration. To make and use an efficient chart will give satisfaction, and memorising and recall like other activities will be subject to intrinsic reinforcement of operant learning. As a map charts the way, so intellectual organisation provides useful knowledge for future exploration.

In the activity of organisation, any or all of past knowledge may be used and as a result of memorisation any or all of acquired knowledge may be available for use in further explorations.

There is an important footnote. If the material to be learned is not interesting, i.e. meaningless, which, of course, it should not be, or a dull but necessary task, then reward, if it be there, will depend not upon intrinsic motivation, but upon some form of social or achievement motivation (cf. chapter, 3, page 35, and chapter 8, page 121). If these are absent then there will be an unwilling and unsuccessful learner, who will not remember.

SUMMARY

The student may summarise by testing his own organisation of the material in this chapter, through a consideration of the following questions.

1. Martin (9 +) is asked to explain an historical wall chart to which he has contributed. He replies that he has forgotten about it and that he doesn't *understand* it now. What are possible reasons for his statement and what would be appropriate actions for his teacher to take?

2. If Robin (12 +) doesn't classify the rock specimens how would you try to find out which of the following statements was true?
   (a) he had not understood the system of classification,
   (b) he had understood but had not memorised,
   (c) he had learned but forgotten,
   (d) he knew, but couldn't be bothered.

3. When her biology teacher suggests revision Mavis (14) says, 'Oh, not that again!' What has gone wrong?

4. Jennie (15) complains, 'I wish we didn't have those two lessons on the same afternoon, I get them all mixed up and forget the

best part of both'. In what circumstances is her complaint justified and why?

5. Does it make sense for Merlin to say, 'I really know but I have just forgotten it.'? Are there better ways of saying what he may possibly mean?

6. How is it that Maggie can remember dates, numbers, and innumerable facts about pop and folk records and very few chemical formulae?

7. What are the possible explanations for Jay's statement, 'I remember it, but I don't know what it means.'

8. Bunty (7) and Merle (11) have written vividly and imaginatively. What are appropriate responses from their teachers? How can the girls be helped with such writing?

The student may, with profit, collect 'howlers' and consider their origin.

NOTES

1. Apart from the brief reference to clinical evidence for stored memories no account has been given in this chapter of the physiological basis for memory; instead there has been only an analogy with a storage or filing system. The omission may be explained by recall of a comment in chapter 2 to the effect that there was considerable speculation about the biological basis of memory storage. However, an attempt will be made here to indicate lines of enquiry and the nature of possible explanations for retention.

Karl S. Lashley spent over thirty years trying to test directly the relation between various parts of the brain and various kinds of memory. Working with rats, monkeys and chimpanzees he would teach an animal a task and then cut or remove a portion of its brain. After recovery from the operation the animal would be tested to find out what it could still remember. Reporting his work in 1950 Lashley wrote (64), 'This series of experiments has yielded a good bit of information about what and where the memory trace is not. It has discovered nothing directly of the real nature of the engram.' (The engram is the name given to the supposed permanent impression left in the brain after experience.) Another line of study has been via electrophysiology. By means of EEG the constant electrical impulses of the brain can be measured. New and more accurate techniques for recording and analysing these impulses are constantly being developed. Gradually it is becoming more possible to analyse electrical impulses occurring during and after learning of specific kinds (38) and progress in this direction should make available more knowledge.

The most recent and promising line of investigation is the biochemical one. Neurochemists have discovered that nerve cells synthesise proteins at a remarkably fast rate. It has also been shown that heightened electrical activity in nerve cells is associated with an increase in the amount of ribonucleic acid (RNA) in them. RNA is vital to the synthesis of proteins and so there is the suggestion that the heightened activity taking place during learning is associated with production of nerve cell proteins, and the further hypothesis that these proteins may be involved in memory storage. Rapid advances are being made in precise analytical methods for discovering the composition of neurons and associated cells, and such methods of investigation are producing evidence to support the proposed hypothesis (60). It will be remembered (note 2, chapter 2) that DNA, the nucleic acid of the chromosomes, is responsible for genetic information, instructions or 'memory', and RNA and proteins play an important part in the way in which the instructions are carried to cells during development. Thus the hypothesis explaining memory storage in terms of protein molecules is an attractive one because it points to a chemical process which may be basic to both genetic and experiential storage systems (cf. chapter 2).

To conclude this note it will be well to remind the reader that rich electrical activity and rich chemical activity are characteristics of the central nervous system. Progress in understanding brain function will depend upon gaining knowledge of the connection between these two forms of activity.

FURTHER READING

Morgan and King (80) is a suitable psychology textbook to read about the following subjects:
S——>S learning, pages 103–109, remembering and forgetting, pages 133–147 and the physiological basis of memory pages 725–731; other standard texts will deal with the same topics. Deese and Hulse (28): chapter 11, though difficult, gives an up-to-date account of experimental work on retention and forgetting; and qualitative changes in memory can be studied in Bartlett (7), a classical study of remembering. Students interested in the effects of repression on forgetting should consult a standard psychological text book of recent date.

Two Pelicans, Hunter (59) and Miller (76, chapter 11) give very interesting and readable accounts of memory, as do the following articles from *Scientific American*: Miller (75) and Underwood (108).

Students interested in the physiological basis of memory may be able to get an idea of the type of work being done by reading the following articles, Hyden (60), Boycott (14) and Jacobson (61) and those who are prepared for more difficult though fascinating study might try Young (118).

Students wishing to study more closely, the relationship between neurological research and educational practice should read Pribram (90).

7 Transfer of Learning and Problem-Solving

In his holiday tent a man who has lived beside a millrace will not lose much sleep from the noise of waves beating on the shore. Earlier habituation will make the new habituation easier. The child who has enjoyed pictures, stories and simple descriptions in the books of the infant school will more readily learn to use the easy reference books of the first junior classes. He will generalise the attitudes gained by conditioning, during his earlier contact with books, and these attitudes will promote easier learning in the new circumstance. The sixth former, who has daily ridden his bicycle across the city from home to school and back, will more quickly learn to manipulate his new motorbike than another seventeen-year-old who has not ridden in traffic and practised applying the highway code. The first youth's already acquired road skill will transfer to and form part of his new skill. It has been seen that memorisation and recall depend upon organisation in relation to past knowledge, and that knowledge is considered useful only if it is readily available for application on further occasions, frequently for further learning. It is thus abundantly clear, as was pointed out at the beginning of chapter 4, that no learning stands on its own, and indeed it is assumed that much of what is learned in school will be useful for later learning. Studies have been made to gain information about the extent to which particular forms of learning may ease the learning of other tasks. Does learning Latin, for example, aid the learning of botany and English, and if so, how? Questions have been asked such as, are some things well worth learning because they will aid a very large amount of future learning? We would all readily agree that to learn to read and write pays high dividends in terms of aiding further study. It is futile to learn things which are neither interesting nor useful in themselves, nor useful in aiding further learning. Are some such studies included in some curricula? Is there perhaps some learning which impedes further learning? For example, do some primary school children learn historical or geographical concepts which will hinder later learning in these subjects? Maps are normally so placed that the north is at the top of the page. But if children learn this fact about maps without understanding more fundamental processes of map-making, may it later be harder for them to learn to make and use maps efficiently? The study of the effect of specific bits of prior learning on the later learning of other special tasks is known as the study of TRANSFER. Transfer from one task to another may of course be zero. For example, to learn Spanish neither helps nor hinders learning to solve quadratic equations. If learning one thing helps the learning of another, transfer is said to be positive. For example a knowledge of O-level mathematics will aid a student studying statistics for use in educational psychology. If learning a particular task hinders the learning of a second one, then transfer is negative. A person who has learned to swim using breast stroke usually experiences negative transfer when he tries to learn the crawl. For centuries educationists have held ideas about the value of various studies; but to answer questions such as those just posed and to know when to expect positive and when negative transfer, controlled investigations have been necessary. Thus, for the past sixty-odd years transfer has been studied in the psychological laboratory and by educational research workers.

EARLY STUDY OF TRANSFER

At the end of the nineteenth century educators were still drawing an analogy between exercising and strengthening particular muscles, thereby improving specific muscular performances and exercising parts of the mind, thereby improving the performance of various mental activities. (The analogy was not, of course, grounded in any sound knowledge of the brain and its activities.) By the analogy it was supposed that certain studies 'strengthened'

G

the memory, others the power of reasoning and so forth; and just as some physical activities may exercise many muscles and produce physical fitness, so it was considered that some studies could produce mental agility, a keen wit or rigorous thinking. Thus rote learning was valued to improve the memory, the repetitious solution of logical and mathematical problems was advocated to strengthen the power of reasoning and some subjects, notably Greek and Latin, were favoured as being beneficial for all-round training of the mind. It was claimed that the study of such subjects gave 'formal or mental discipline', by training the reason and powers of observation, comparison and synthesis.

It will come as no surprise to those who have read the last chapter that the first of these ideas to be questioned was that rote learning improved future memory. In 1890 William James, brother of novelist Henry, and one of the 'fathers of psychology', decided to test the very limited hypothesis that rote learning of one poem would aid the rote learning of another. He recorded the time which he took, during an 8 day period, to memorise 158 lines of French verse. During the next 38 days he practised learning *Paradise Lost* for 20 minutes each day. He then learned another 158 lines from the original poem. It took him longer than before. Some of James' students carried out similar trials. A few showed some gain in learning time on the final task, but there was no significant gain for the group. The theory that exercising the faculty of memory improved future memorisation had not stood up to the first direct test. Although subsequent tests showed that sometimes practice led to quicker memorisation of the same kind of material, controlled experiments during the next thirty years indicated that little automatic transfer took place between memorising tasks of different kinds (117, chapter 24). It was not until 1927 that H. Woodrow (116) conducted an experiment which tested the hypothesis that there might be procedures for effective memorising which could be learned. 108 students were divided into three groups, known as the control, the practice and the experimental group. All three groups learned and were tested on six memory tasks: rote poetry, rote prose, historical dates, Turkish–English vocabulary, lists of consonants and the substance of factual material. The control group had no further practice in memorising; the practice group spent 177 minutes learning tasks similar to the original ones; the experimental group spent 177 minutes divided between learning how to go about memorising and trying to put the recommendations into practice. (The recommendations were similar to but less detailed than those outlined in the last chapter, page 79.) All three groups then learned and were tested on another task similar to the first one. There was little difference between the scores of the control and practice groups and neither had made much improvement upon their first scores; however, the experimental group who had received training in memorising showed a very substantial gain in their scores. Early theorists had evidently been wrong to suppose that exercising the memory would automatically improve further memorising, but here was evidence that memorising was a skill which could be learned and then practised in relation to varied tasks.

In 1901 two famous experimental psychologists, E. L. Thorndike and R. S. Woodworth, seriously questioned the ideas of formal discipline and sought experimental evidence by which to confirm or refute them. Their first experiments were designed to find out whether learning to make accurate observations of one kind of material would lead to easier learning in further observational tasks. In one experiment subjects practised estimating the areas of rectangles which varied from 10–100 sq. cms. After each estimate the correct area was given and, as would be expected, immediate knowledge of results led to improvement. The learning continued until an agreed standard had been reached. Before and after this learning the subjects were given a test in estimating the areas of different-sized rectangles, triangles and varied shapes. Similar experiments were carried out where subjects were given practice in estimating lengths and weights accompanied by pre- and post-tests on different but analogous material.

The results of the group of experiments may be summed up by saying that although in some cases improvement from pre- to post-test was shown, yet it was very variable and seldom as great as the improvement on the practised task (104). In so far as transfer effects were shown, they were attributed by the experimenters to specific methods and habits that were carried from the practice series to the test, and such factors could lead to positive or negative transfer. For example, one subject realised during the learning session that he had a tendency to over-estimate the areas with which he was working and he learned to correct this tendency. He continued to apply his correction when estimating the larger areas of the test series, but this proved a mistaken policy for his over-estimation was less great for the larger areas and the net result was under-estimation of them. As in the case of James' memory investigation, this work led to further experiments. Thorndike summed up the findings in his books of 1903 and 1913. He said that transfer takes place if there are factors common to the original learning task and the task which is facilitated. These common elements may be in the material to be learned or in the procedures of learning, but common factors there must be. In the first case, learning A makes the learning of B easier, because B has already been partly learned by studying A, as in the example already given of O-level maths aiding the study of statistics. In the second case, learning B is easier because the learner already knows how to set about the task; for example, the procedures for using a reference book, once learned, can be applied to the use of bibliographies, dictionaries, encyclopaedias, cookery books, technicians' manuals, almanacs, etc., and aid many learning tasks.

Another early educational psychologist, C. H. Judd, in 1908 carried out a now famous experiment in which boys threw darts at an underwater target. Judd claimed that this experiment provided evidence of an important factor operating in some cases of transfer, namely, the generalisation and application of a known principle to a specific task. Unfortunately, Judd did not report the full details of the experiment nor give details of the scores made by the boys.

For this reason, in 1941 (51) a similar experiment was designed and carried out. 90 fourteen-year-old boys of above average intelligence were divided into three equal groups known as A, B and control groups. Groups A and B were given a written explanation of the principles of refraction accompanied by a diagram which showed that an object under water is not in the place where it appears to be. The boys were allowed to study the explanation until they were confident that they understood it. Group B's explanation sheets contained one more sentence than the sheets given to group A. This sentence stated that the deeper the water, the further the distance of the object from its apparent position. The control group were given no preparatory explanations at all. All three groups fired with a fifty shot repeater airgun at a rifle target submerged 6″ below water and they continued until they had hit the target three times in succession. The target was then raised by 4″ and the process repeated. In both trials, the control group required most shots to reach the criterion of success and group B the least. For each group, the average number of trials required on the second test was approximately three less than on the first one. When the exact records are statistically tested it is found that, according to present-day standards of rigour, there can be reasonable confidence that in only one of these cases the differences are not due to chance. The difference between the scores of group B and the control group on the second task is the only significant difference and so the experiment provides evidence for only one of a number of possible conclusions, namely, that the additional information given to group B gave them an advantage in transfer over the control group. Both A and B groups were given the general principle of refraction, but group B, by being told *the deeper the water the more distant the object from its image*, had been shown how the principle operated in relation to the movement of the target. From the evidence of this experiment, therefore, it would appear that a practical task, at any rate for these fourteen-year-olds, was not made easier simply by knowledge of a general principle. Before the principle could be applied there had to be additional knowledge of its relevance in the special circumstance, and this represents some modification of Judd's original hypothesis. Clearly this is a matter of some importance to teachers and it will be considered again in the light of further evidence and enquiry.

The student may have recognised that these initial studies of transfer, like the first experimental studies of simple learning, marked the beginning of empirical psychology. Sceptical of the nebulous theories of mental disciplines, the early educational psychologists made experimental attacks on the problem of transfer. The unresolved questions which their work produced gave direction to further studies.

LATER STUDIES OF TRANSFER

Two questions follow directly from the earlier work:

1. Are there some procedures which direct methods of learning and which will be of aid in numerous modes of learning?
2. Can transfer be predicted by locating common factors in different tasks?

In addition, studies related to transfer via the appreciation of general principles have been of two main kinds. Firstly, there has been study of *learning sets* which transfer from certain situations to other similar ones and facilitate understanding. Secondly, there has been considerable study of the generalisation and application of principles in relation to problem solving. These four related topics and their relevance to teaching must be considered.

COMMON PROCEDURES FOR LEARNING

Probably the most common skill used in all learning situations is memorising, and since the experimental work of the twenties there has been considerable increase in the understanding of the memory process which has led to the detailed recommendations for memorising given in the last chapter. As Thorndike pointed out, there are other skills common to many learning procedures, and once learned they can be transferred to many learning situations. The skill of using reference books has already been mentioned and there are other similar skills such as using maps, charts, and graphs which, once acquired, can be used in relation to the learning of many subjects: geography, history, botany, economics, etc. Once a student has learned to use laboratory apparatus in an elementary science course, he will be better able to carry out the more complicated experimental work required in more advanced courses. The reader may think of other such useful techniques which may be transferred from one learning task to another. It is obvious that teachers must provide opportunities for pupils to master those procedures which are important for continued learning.

ANALYSIS OF COMMON ELEMENTS IN TASKS

One way of analysing tasks is into their stimulus and response components and for some tasks this makes prediction of transfer possible. As a simple example consider driving a car. A competent owner-driver through operant learning has acquired an habitual pattern of responses to a given set of stimuli: steering wheel, gear lever, clutch pedal, accelerator and the assemblage on the dashboard. Now remove him from the family saloon and put him in a lorry driver's cab. He will surely learn to drive the lorry more easily than one who has never driven a car before, and this indicates some positive transfer, but how does he set about his task? He will look carefully at the dashboard array and after noting their positions he will cautiously begin to drive. It takes him some time to get used to the new position of the gear lever, and to adjust to the feel of the brakes and steering wheel, so there is some negative transfer. In sum, however, we should estimate gain rather than loss as a result of his earlier learning. How can the stimulus response components of these tasks be compared? The stimuli of the second task are not *identical* with those of the first, the stimulus items may be in different places, be larger, stiffer, heavier, etc., but they are *similar* and the responses which must be made to them are the same, e.g. pressing the clutch at gear change, etc. Here is exemplified an important principle of transfer, namely, *if responses are constant, transfer will be a function of the degree of similarity between stimuli*. (The reader should recognise here that this type of transfer is an extension of the principle of stimulus generalisation described earlier.) Transfer was positive and there would be considerable gain in learning time when the driver transferred from car to lorry, but put him in the cockpit of a plane and though he may still learn more quickly than one who has never driven any vehicle there will be less positive transfer because the stimuli are less similar to those in his car, and there will be far less positive transfer if we expect him to manipulate the controls of a space capsule.

In these two cases, only some of the loss of positive transfer will be due to less similarity between the stimuli in the old and new situations. A new factor will have become important; namely, there will be the need to change responses and we are thus led to the second principle of transfer. *If the responses in the transfer task are different from those in the original task, then the greater the similarity of stimuli, the less the transfer.*

These two principles of transfer may be conveniently illustrated by considering a set of alternative changes in the usual system of traffic lights. We may then examine the operation of transfer as a driver learns to respond to any one of the new systems. For the first series of changes the colour signal for *stop* will alter from red through a series until green means *stop*. For the second, the response to red will be altered to *go* and then signals will change through orange until green again indicates *go*. These changes and their transfer effects can probably best be shown by means of a diagram.

First series of changes				Second series of changes
Response: Stop		Colour signals:		Response: Go
Original response	S1	Red	S1	Opposite response *Maximum negative transfer*
Decreasing positive transfer	S2	Orange Red	S2	Decreasing negative transfer
	S3	Orange	S3	
	S4	Orange Yellow	S4	
Increasing negative transfer	S5	Yellow	S5	Increasing positive Transfer
	S6	Yellow Green	S6	
Opposite response *Maximum negative transfer*	S7	Green	S7	Original response

From the table it is easy to see that it would be relatively easy to *stop* at orange and to *go* at yellow green. It would be very difficult to *go* at red and to *stop* at green where maximum negative transfer is operating, e.g. opposite response to identical stimulus. The reader may estimate the amount of positive or negative transfer likely to be present when a driver adapts to any one of the possibilities presented.

The two principles of transfer illustrated by the above example may appear very obvious to the reader, but there is nothing as clear as hindsight, and in fact, many learning situations, both inside and outside school, require complex analysis because they combine many stimuli and responses which together influence transfer. Controlled laboratory studies, using measurable materials including familiar nonsense syllables and careful experimental designs, have been required to provide evidence for the stated principles, and interested students should consult the further reading list. Here it will be sufficient to consider the application of this type of task analysis to school work, showing how the principle of positive transfer may operate to facilitate learning. It will be best to begin with an example. Suppose that some nine-year-old children have earlier reached the stage of making and using simple block graphs for recording and reading off information. Suppose that they have used 'units' on the horizontal axis which can be placed in any order; e.g. makes of cars passing school, television programmes watched by class members, etc. It will now be easy for a teacher to encourage the making of a graph where the units to be used on the horizontal axis are numbers which need to be set in order before recording. Next it is an easy progression to a step graph, that is, a block graph representing an algebraic relationship, e.g. a block graph to represent a given multiplication table. From such a block graph it is an easy transition to a column graph. Suppose that the column graph represents the table of threes. The children can *see* that the tops of the columns are in a straight line, they can join these tops and they will have drawn a straight line graph expressing the relationship $y = 3x$, and they will be able then to draw this line without the columns.

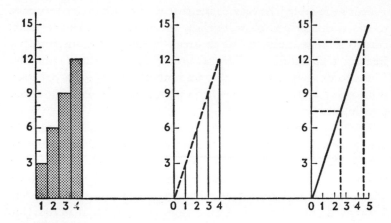

The children will not necessarily be ready to express the relationship y = 3x in this symbolic way, but by looking at their graphs they will probably be able to read from them information such as $4\frac{1}{2} \times 3$ or $7\frac{1}{2} \div 3$. It is clear that in drawing and reading from the graph of the straight line y = 3x the children have performed an entirely new task. They have learned to do this easily by the operation of the principles of positive transfer. Three different kinds of block graph were made without recording responses being changed in any major way and so no difficulties are experienced in the transition from making at first a pictorial block graph and finally a column graph expressing an algebraic relationship; but the transition made possible a new way of seeing and reading records; that is, a new way of using stimuli to obtain information. Because the stimuli are changed gradually, no difficulty is experienced in changing from reading from separate blocks or columns to reading from a line, at first seen to join the tops of columns, Children who learn so, will later more readily understand conversion graphs and gradients (3 times table gives a gradient of 3 in 1). Through further positive transfer, in the secondary school they will meet the expression y = mx + c with greater comprehension than children who meet it for the first time. Teachers who are aware of the value of positive transfer, will be alert to notice when it is possible to analyse learned tasks so that they can be constantly used to lead on to new skills, discoveries and interests. Such analysis should direct grading and sequence of work in the classroom and it is perhaps best exemplified in the careful construction of the graded sequences of programmed learning texts.

Many complex skills and much knowledge are derived by combining, in a new pattern, already acquired knowledge or skills. One important way of ensuring positive transfer in learning is to give many opportunities for combining past elements in new ways. In order to do this, teachers must not only be aware of important combinations but must also be able to motivate children to use their several skills or their accumulated knowledge in more difficult combinations.

Many children can write interestingly, write neatly and spell and punctuate correctly if they are asked to perform these items of a writer's craft separately. How can children be helped to combine them into a satisfactory and satisfying whole? Children may learn many mathematical skills and gain many mathematical ideas in the maths workshop. A good teacher will want to find a way by which the children can use these ideas and skills together in an exciting new piece of learning. Perhaps they can find an explanation for a working model. After learning a number of different scientific principles, could an opportunity for positive transfer be afforded by encouraging the children to invent simple working models? It is this type of educational problem to which a knowledge of transfer draws attention.

LEARNING SETS

The concept of learning set in relation to transfer originated from H. F. Harlow and the best introduction to this topic is via some of Harlow's experimental work. Harlow gave a very long series of learning tasks to groups of rhesus monkeys (45) (46). A monkey sits behind a tray on which he is offered two objects differing in size, colour and shape, say a blue cube and a red cone. The objects are placed one on each side of the tray and under one of them, known as the correct object, say the blue cube, there are nuts and raisins. The monkey chooses one of the objects and if he chooses the correct one he is rewarded by the food. The process is then repeated. The reward is always under the blue cube but, of course, the position of the two objects on the tray must be varied randomly so that the monkey does not learn simply to choose one position on the tray. When the monkey has learned to choose the right object all, or nearly all, the time the task is changed, another similar task being given. For example, now the animal may have to choose between a green cylinder and a black hemisphere.

Eight tasks all similar to the two mentioned were given to the eight monkeys and the graph, marked 1–8, shows their progress for the first six trials when learning this group of tasks.

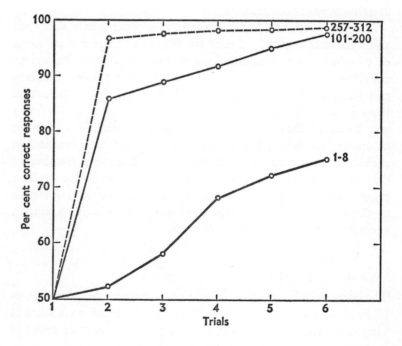

Of course, the monkeys have absolutely no cue for the first choice of any task and, as one would expect from chance, about 50% of their first choices are correct and 50% wrong. After this first choice it can be seen that there is a continuous improvement and we can say that the monkeys are gradually learning how to make this relatively simple choice. Harlow did not stop here; he went on, and in all taught the monkeys over three hundred such tasks. The graphs of the results for the first six trials of tasks 101–200 and tasks 257–312 are shown. It is immediately clear from the graphs that the monkeys learn the later tasks much more quickly than the earlier ones. After the first chance choice, in the last group of tasks, the monkeys are making nearly 100% correct choice and they no longer learn the task gradually. Harlow reports that following the first blind choice some of the monkeys solved from 20 to 30 consecutive problems *with no errors whatever*. When, through training, new problems, of a type which were initially difficult, can be solved easily or at once, then the learner is said to have acquired *a learning set* for these tasks. Alternatively, it may be said that he has *learned how to learn* tasks of this particular kind. Harlow arranged for similar discrimination tasks to be given to a group of nursery school children. It was found that, although most of the children worked more quickly than the monkeys, their learning followed the same pattern and the graph of their results looked much like that of the monkeys' results. Harlow does note, however, that the brighter monkeys learned faster than the duller children.

Harlow trained the same monkeys on further groups of more difficult tasks. The first group of tasks were discrimination-reversal problems. In these tasks, after a certain number of trials the reward was switched to the alternative object, and the monkeys had to reverse their choice. Harlow reports that although one would expect this set of problems to be more difficult for the monkeys, nevertheless they were learned more rapidly than the earlier tasks. The previously acquired learning set to *shift choice when wrong*, aided the learning of these more difficult tasks; in other words, possessing a learning set led to *positive transfer*. The children also did these tasks and their results showed the effects of greater positive transfer than was shown for the monkeys.

In another group of tasks there were three objects to choose from and the correct one was always the odd one. Sometimes a pair were alike in shape, sometimes in colour and sometimes in size, but the correct one was always the one which differed from these two. Again the monkeys learned to do the tasks, even when it meant a complete reversal of their behaviour, that is when an identical block changed from being the correct choice in one task to being one of the pair and therefore incorrect in the next task. (It is interesting that Harlow likened this learning to the learning of a child beginning to use the words *I, you,* and *he,* when the meaning of the word changes according to the speaker. When the child speaks, *I* refers to himself, *you* to the person addressed and *he* to some third person. However, when the child is addressed, the child is no longer *I* but *you.*)

Another group of tasks were even more difficult. Again there were three objects but now two of the three were alike in colour and two alike in shape. For example, a trio could be a red U shape block, a green U shape block and a red X shape. The monkey learned to choose the one with the odd colour if the objects were presented on an orange tray, and the one with the odd shape if they were presented on a cream tray. By working at these problems the monkeys acquired a learning set to choose the odd one and positive transfer was noted. What the monkeys had done was to solve a super-problem. In addition to learning to shift choice they had learned to recognise oddness in different circumstances, and under different guises. *Learning sets* may be thought of as adaptations to relationships which will be sought in other appropriate contexts. It is suggested that in much of their learning, human beings make such adaptations and that the learning sets so formed lead to positive transfer in later learning. In chapter 6, page 81, it was stressed that organised memorisation and formal thinking follow upon experiential acquisition of the necessary concepts and linguistic skills. It is here suggested that, similarly, children making first-hand observations and discoveries are acquiring learning sets for later use. Thus if a primary school child learns, from his own observations and from experiments at the nature bench, that light, air and water each affect the healthy growth of plants, then he is also acquiring a learning set to perceive, at a later stage and in a wider context, the relationship between growth and environmental conditions. In other words, although not yet ready to do so formally, he is *learning how to learn* biological science, for he is acquiring a set towards the relationships inherent in the structure of the subject. New movements for curriculum development are partially prompted by this hypothesis that early learning sets can lead to positive transfer in later learning. Thus the Nuffield Mathematics Project for primary school children is based on the supposition that children can 'gain some insight into the nature of the subject' (85), that is to say, appreciate the structure of the subject by *learning how to learn* it. In *The Process of Education*, J. S. Bruner discusses the findings of a conference of psychologists, subject specialists and gifted teachers, concerned with curriculum development (17). He speaks of the *spiral curriculum* which turns back on itself, and among other things he is referring to the necessity for giving ample opportunity at the bottom of the spiral for children to develop appropriate learning sets and *learn how to learn* what will later be required. It would be a mistake, however, to suppose that learning sets are only acquired in early years; their acquisition is a continuous process and hence the spiral metaphor. For example, college students who come to the study of psychology with learning sets derived from recent studies of other biological sciences, are ready to look for, understand and appreciate genetic and evolutionary principles where these are relevant to their new study. For students not familiar with such biological thought the new subject may, at first, be more difficult; but for these students, this study may be the origin of a new learning set, to be used later for positive transfer in other learning. When there has been time to evaluate the new curricula there will be new evidence to support or refute the theory of learning sets and transfer by *learning how to learn*.

LEARNING AND PROBLEM-SOLVING

To make a satisfactory study of problem-solving would necessitate a study of cognitive development and thinking in all its diversity and individuality. This is of course beyond the scope of this book and only some few of the relationships between learning and problem-solving will be considered. At the outset it is necessary to draw a distinction between learning *by* problem-solving and learning *to* solve problems.

Living creatures are active and curious (chapter 3, page 29). Youngsters continuously experiment and ask to find answers to how? and why? It is problems, rather than heaven, that lie around us in our infancy! As children gradually acquire concepts, knowledge, and thus expectations, they begin to direct their questions chiefly towards instances which in some way lie outside the expected framework, or the events which conflict with accepted suppositions. As was stressed in chapter 3 (page 32), such puzzlement is a powerful motive for learning and leads to problem-solving or discovery methods of learning. In chapter 6 (page 81) the necessity for learning with understanding was stressed and recommendations were made for bringing it about. The first three of these (page 81) depend upon a problem-solving approach to learning, where children with guidance both *supply the questions, seek, and with help find, the answers*. In this chapter it has been seen that such methods are valuable in creating learning sets which lead to the appreciation of the structure of the subjects studied. If much of learning is to progress by means of discovering and solving problems, then teachers need to know how to direct such activities. Judd's early work was an attempt to investigate one way of promoting efficient problem-solving and since the follow-up work of 1941 there have been a number of investigations into the effect upon immediate problem-solving, and upon transfer, of knowing in advance the principle required for solution. Evidence is inconclusive as to which of the following procedures is the more satisfactory:

(a) knowing in advance the principle required;
(b) being given leads as to how to find such a principle;
(c) being given information about the way in which a principle can be applied to the problem (as for group B in previous example);
(d) being left without guidance to work out the principle needed.

Although each of the studies was carried out with homogeneous groups, they sampled people of different age groups who would therefore be at different stages of cognitive development and probably show variation in the number of available learning sets. (See reading list, page 114.) I would suggest that in classroom conditions the teacher must on each occasion take into account the previous experience and knowledge of the learners, before deciding on how much and what kind of help they need. If learning sets in relation to the new problem are well established, then little help will be required, but if they are not, then many leads will have to come from the teacher. On no account should lack of guidance lead to the problems becoming so vague or so difficult that the children can gain no satisfaction from their solution. Should this happen, then the supposed power of the enterprise, intrinsic motivation of genuine curiosity, would be destroyed. Perhaps another of the results of teacher-research into new curricula will be that more evidence will accrue about the best way of directing children's discovery and problem-solving.

There is another important and practical matter to be studied in relation to problem-solving, namely, rigidity of fixation which was mentioned at the beginning of chapter 6. I am sure that many readers will have had the experience of approaching a difficulty over and over again in the *same* way. One says, 'I can't see why –' or 'I can't get a solution' and then is shown how to look at the question in a *new* way. Many well-reported and interesting investigations have been made to try to find out the causes of such fixedness. (See further reading list, page 115.) The important question for teachers is, can children be trained so that such rigidity is minimised? There have been several attempts to provide experimental evidence on this topic and though results are suggestive rather than conclusive, it will be profitable to consider a summary and experiment made in 1958 (1). Two equally matched groups of 11–12-year-old children were trained to solve the same problems (water jar problems where given volumes had to be measured with limited available measures). One group was shown two ways of solving each problem. When the children were tested on similar problems and on different ones (jig-saw type paper and pencil tasks) the two-method group offered more varied solutions and persevered longer to find varied solutions than did the other group. Summing up their own and other people's work the experimenters say that a teacher's consistent training in alternative solutions to problems may result in efficient overcoming of rigidity.

In conclusion it must be remembered that in chapter 6 stress

H

was placed on the unity of the learning process. After understand-ing has been given by discovery and problem-solving methods, then it is necessary for the learner to solve another problem, e.g. how best to fix this new knowledge in his own memory. Unless this is done (see recommendations 5–8, chapter 6, page 82) the learner will not be in a position, later on, to use his learning sets for further study. He may at that time, of course, use books, or other sources, to gain knowledge, but he will need to remember from his past learning in order to know what is relevant and required.

There are fashions, without rational justification, in educational methods as well as elsewhere. At times the slogan has been: *cram in the facts, teach skills and the problems will take care of themselves*; and at other times: *never mind the facts and skills, teach the kids to solve problems and discover answers and then they will learn facts and skills for themselves*. Both slogans are equally inadequate. Motiva-tion to pose questions, knowledge, skills, learning sets to dis-criminate what is wanted *now*, and problem-solving skills, all are necessary. Alone neither slogan is sufficient.

SUMMARY

To summarise this chapter, and test his knowledge of it, the student should endeavour to:
1. Answer all the questions posed in the opening section;
2. Give convincing arguments against both the slogans quoted in the last paragraph.

FURTHER READING

Ellis (30) gives a clear summary and sample papers relating to transfer. Interested students could examine a selection of papers illustrative of points made in this chapter, and might also look at Wittrock and Twelker (115). A fairly difficult but up-to-date account of transfer is given in Deese and Hulse (28).

A very easily read book on problem-solving in the classroom is Hudgins (58), and students might well follow up some of the references given at the end of each chapter. Williams (113) is also useful on this topic.

Students wishing to follow further the connection between discovery, problem-solving, creative thinking and classroom procedure could read Getzels (39) or Torrance (107), and the books by Bruner (17) and (18) mentioned in the text. The article by Bibergall (12) and the useful list of references could be studied with profit.

A fascinating book on the subject of problem-solving is Polya (91). As an example of the assessment of evidence on methods of learning in schools in this country the student may examine Gooch and Kellmer-Pringle (40).

Students should study new movements for curriculum reform in subjects which interest them.

8 Learners and Teachers

'The relation between the one who instructs and the one who is instructed is never indifferent in its effects upon learning.'

J. S. Bruner, *Theorems for a theory of instruction* (19)

To most teachers, the 'theorem' will read as understatement. Motivation, conditioning, operant learning, reinforcement, remembering, forgetting, transfer, discovery, problem-solving, all these processes, separately and together, can generate success or failure; and most teachers believe that it is interaction between learner and teacher which determines accomplishment or stalemate. It is unfortunate that holding this correct belief, but mistaking a necessary for a sufficient condition, some teachers have assumed that ability to gain rapport with children is a substitute for understanding learning processes. Happily, 'an encouraging number of teachers are beginning to concern themselves with theories of learning . . .' (*Plowden Report* (23, paragraph 518)) and an attempt will here be made to draw attention to factors closely connected with teacher–pupil relationships which effectively promote certain educational goals. Consideration will be given to methods by which teachers may lead pupils towards: (1) acceptable self-imposed standards; and (2) lasting interests and enduring enquiry.

ACQUIRING STANDARDS AND SELF-JUDGEMENT

Apart from disliking the air of patronage implicit in 'Good boy!' readers may see little difference between this form of praise and the statement, 'That's good!' The important difference is that the latter remark appeals to a different source of emotional satisfaction from the former. As is so often the case, light can be thrown on the matter by observation of young children at play. A glowing smile of satisfaction may be seen on a toddler's face as he achieves some simple task; fixing a piece into his new puzzle frame, opening a door for the first time, etc.; and that smile will be joyous even when the child is unaware of the presence of anyone else. A learner is said to be involved in a task when he is working towards such pleasure in achievement. It is equally true that junior will imitate elder brother and Dad because he wants to be like them and he will smile with delight when they praise him and he thinks that his competence has made him *one of them*. Human beings are motivated both towards group membership (social motives of chapter 3, page 35) and towards achievement. Both goals can lead to self-esteem and sometimes, as with junior, the goals are closely linked.

As children grow older, the tasks which they must learn become more complex and so it becomes more difficult for them to judge their own competence and they look to others for help in judgement. Now self-esteem derived from competence can be confused with self-esteem derived from the acceptance and approval of those to whom one turns for standards. In this chapter, it will be suggested that parents and teachers should endeavour to minimise this confusion. A child should not feel that his parent or his teacher love, like or value him less, because his maths is 'middlin' or his musical progress slow; but if he does feel so, then ANXIETY over the esteem in which he is held will distract him from involvement in his tasks and his learning will be the poorer. Granted that teacher-pupil rapport has been established and that the class is working as a social group (cf. chapter 3, page 35) how can teachers minimise the confusion?

Anxiety

From reading recommended in chapter 3 students should know that members of any class or group will, according to their previous experience, respond variously to the approaches of their teacher. The youngster used to voluble praises from mother, or previous teacher, may interpret a quiet teacher's more subdued responses as critical or disapproving; while a child accustomed to perpetual nagging may suppose the same response to be appreciative. Teachers need to be aware of such individual differences. Perceptive teachers usually are, and try to deal with them before they give rise to difficulties (frequently to anxieties). The above example illustrates, very simply, the importance of anxiety as a factor in learning. The second child is anxious before he starts and will be likely to attack tasks with caution, for fear of evoking displeasure. The first child, in the absence of customary fulsome praise becomes unnecessarily anxious. Both children, because anxious, are likely to become over-dependent upon the teacher, paying more attention to her reaction to them, than to the task in hand, and thus their learning efficiency will be decreased.

In recent years, recognition of the important relationship between anxiety and learning has led to considerable research on the topic, but the relationship has proved complex and it has not yet been fully explored. The basic effect of anxiety upon learning can, however, be understood by reference to the arousal function of emotions and the cue function of stimuli which were explained in chapter 3, pages 27 and 28. Anxiety is related to fear, and in this context may be regarded as a permanent or semi-permanent state of uneasiness due to fear of disapproval and/or failure. When an individual is learning some task he is motivated, or aroused, to attend to certain cue-stimuli, i.e. the stimuli of the task. If this motivation is heightened beyond a certain level, it will interfere with efficient attention to cues. It is suggested that states of high anxiety increase arousal so that cue stimuli cannot be readily interpreted and learning is made difficult. On this hypothesis it would be expected that disruptive effects of anxiety would be more quickly noticed when cue stimuli are complex and less likely to occur when the task is relatively simple. Experimental evidence supports this suggestion for highly anxious learners (anxiety measured through physiological states, cf. chapter 3, page 28, or by results of a questionnaire) tend to do as well as, if not slightly better than, low-anxious learners of matched ability when the task is simple, but less well when it is complex. Other experiments have shown that it is not only the complexity of the task but also the accompanying instructions which will lead to differences in performance between learners at high and low levels of anxiety. Exhortations to finish on time, to do better than X etc., and test situations tend to lower the capabilities of the highly anxious. The low-anxious groups are not so affected, and if the task is simple, their performance may even improve as a result of the instructions. For anxious students it is not surprising that decrement in learning occurs, since, as in the case of the dependent youngsters of the first example, attention is drawn from the task to the consequences of it, and to success or failure for the learner. It has also been shown that interruptions to a learning task tend to decrease the efficiency of the highly anxious, more than that of the low-anxious groups. In summary, it appears that, for all but the simplest tasks, *external* pressures of any kind will cause anxious students to lose ground. For more detailed discussion and experimental evidence relating to the last two paragraphs, see (25), (52), (63), (87) and (103, page 416).

Practising teachers and students who, from earlier chapters of this book have appreciated the importance to learning of motivation and reinforcement, will know that a child should not be placed in a position where he *cannot* learn a given task and where he lacks the ability to attain some competence. It is to avoid such a contingency that primary school groups fluctuate, and are flexible within a larger class unit, while in secondary schools there are frequently subject sets, and in both, there is a proportion of individual work. Granted a framework which permits tasks appropriate to individual learners, what can now be said about reinforcement and evaluation of learning designed to minimise disruptive anxiety? In chapter 5, page 60, it was made clear that knowledge of results is an integral part of the learning process implying careful grading and useful as well as rewarding feedback. It should now be possible to see that in addition, for all but the simplest tasks, evaluation of set goals needs to be given in relation to *the task* rather than to its consequences for the learner. Thus the way teachers give praise and criticism becomes very important.
Examples:

1. Praise a child for his successful use of skill, rather than for his success, especially competitive success.
   'Thank you George, we can all easily read your clear and neat label' rather than, 'George has made the best label' or just 'Good'.

2. When knowledge is required, 'Listen to *what Andrea has found out*', rather than, 'Listen to Andrea'.
3. When there is a problem, '*David's suggestion is a good one because* we can now find out whether . . .'.
4. After creative work, 'Let's look at/listen to/enjoy the picture/poem/story which *Patricia has made*'.

When praising individual work, rather than shared work, the emphasis is likely to be more on task progress and improvement of work methods and here too there will be more involvement and less apprehension when praise and criticism are both divorced from social acceptance.

A child who has learned to associate praise with competence in specific tasks will be less likely to feel that his personality is being criticised when he must be told that his work is not good enough; but it is, of course, when criticism is given that it is especially important to maintain an agreeable social relationship. 'We shan't be able to read that small writing, shall we?' said agreeably, is likely to produce, 'Can I have another card?' with self-esteem intact. But, 'Oh Georgina, you are a poor writer' may lead to anxious tears or silent reflection on, 'I am the group's bad writer', a role which may be accepted and lived with. Thus it is not only the anxious who benefit from the proposed policy; there are advantages to all, in that undesirable roles are not so easily assumed. 'I am good, I needn't bother', shows an attitude less likely to be developed by continual reference to rising standards than by variations on, 'Good! Andrew', 'Well done! Andrew', 'Listen to Andrew' etc.

In my own experience nowhere has the diminution of disruptive anxiety been more apparent than when students learning to teach become involved in the task of helping young learners, rather than continually considering assessment of themselves as teachers. In accordance with the policy advocated, involvement in the task has been encouraged by tutorial discussion and evaluation of children's learning and work, i.e. by evaluation of what in this case are the task products. When anxiety is reduced standards rise.

Frustration

A barrier which impedes progress towards a goal frustrates; that is, it causes heightened emotional reactions. A difficulty in learning or problem-solving either in the task or in the conditions of working is such a barrier and the extent and type of emotional reaction experienced by the learner will determine the quality of his learning. If the extent of the difficulty is such that great stress is felt, then this heightened emotional tone, will, as in other circumstances, disrupt cue function. Such failure can be avoided by the careful grading constantly advocated. Rigidity in problem-solving may sometimes result from fixation on few cues because stress has disrupted perception of the whole. (See reading list for chapter 7.) When stress is less severe, some studies show (16) that introducing frustration into a learning situation can increase the vigour of responses, while one experiment using college students (37) showed that some students, frustrated in a task, quickly blame themselves for failure and give up. The study of frustration is complex, but in this context it may be tentatively suggested that it will be anxious students with a generalised worry about possible failure who will tend to withdraw, while those with attention centred upon carrying out the task will be likely to press on, perhaps with added effort. Such a suggestion indicates that the policy for evaluation already advocated would be beneficial in increasing ability to tolerate frustration, a necessary attribute if learners are later to work independently and set their own standards.

Coping or Defending?

A learner is coping with a problem when he is viewing all the relevant evidence, assessing it, and using it. A learner is coping with a skill when he is carefully taking note of all available corrective feedback; and he is coping with memorising, when he is mindful of all the steps outlined in chapter 5. In other words, if the learner is involved in the task, he will be coping in order to achieve competence. If, however, the learner is anxiously fearful of loss of favour his reaction to difficulty will be not coping, but face-saving in an attempt to protect the esteem which he is fearful of losing. When children make defensive attempts to save face, they hide their difficulties and it becomes increasingly harder for teachers to explain and help. To lessen the crippling disadvantages of defensive learning is one of the greatest gains from a method of praise which separates recognition of competence from social approval.

Appreciative judgement

Anxiety, frustration and face-saving are reduced and standards raised by separating praise for performance from personal praise. But this is not all. When children are introduced to public standards of judgement, they are not only helped towards task involvement, but also by associating pleasurable praise with evaluation they begin to develop their own standard of judgement and they can start judging their own work. As soon as children have some appreciation of qualitative standard, then they can enjoy achievement wherever it is found and they can begin to appreciate each other's work. Now an exciting story, a well-designed experiment, athletic prowess, a moving poem, these will be judged by appropriate criteria and valued both by achievers and by appreciative classmates. In terms of learning transfer perhaps such activities may be thought of as providing learning sets which will lead to critical appreciation in later study as well as to self-set standards.

ENDURING ENQUIRY AND INTERESTS

It seems not unreasonable to hope that after 10–17 years of schooling most people will have acquired some lasting interests, and few would deny that the promotion of such interests is a sound educational aim. But it would usually be thought that another mark of an educated man is his readiness to be interested, so that he is open to new experiences and new branches of learning; and able to recognise and attempt solution of problems when he meets them. Such qualities are implied when it is said that a man shows enduring enquiry. Both lasting interests and enduring enquiry result from the cognitive motive of curiosity, the extreme importance of which was emphasised in chapter 3, page 32, and again in chapters 6 and 7. This motive, no less than the motive towards achievement, is closely associated with social motivation, and the connection has important consequences for educational practice.

The socially motivated learner not infrequently IDENTIFIES himself with, and takes his goals from, an admired person (cf. chapter 3, page 35). If teachers show lively curiosity about, enthusiasm for, and interest in, the problems, topics and subjects which are learned in their classrooms, then it is likely that learners will catch this enthusiasm, become emotionally involved, and carry their interest with them long after the courses are over. (cf. chapter 4, conditioning of emotions.)

The teacher of young children needs a lively appreciation of the world around him, for as a model, he must enhance, not lessen, the children's sense of wonder. 'As children, we invest the world with value and it is the job of education to return our investment with interest' (81). The teacher in the middle school years, perhaps as one of a team, may begin to offer special skills and knowledge to help in the solution of problems. 'A great discovery solves a great problem but there is a grain of discovery in the solution of any problem' (91). In the later years of education, the teacher will be looked upon as expert in his own field. A learner fortunate enough to have enjoyed, at each level, a succession of stimulating teachers will very probably have acquired the intellectual liveliness of enduring enquiry, and a combination of social, cognitive and achievement motivation should have led to some special competences and consequent enduring interests. Aesthetic appreciation, intellectual curiosity, respect for varieties both of knowledge and thought, zest for experience, these are only some of the qualities which go to make a stimulating teacher; and they imply high standards for teacher education.

It is necessary to consider a little further pupil-teacher collaboration which can lead to an open mind and enduring enquiry. D. E. Berlyne in an essay on intrinsic motivation (10) has analysed this characteristic of an educated man along the following lines. Of a man with this quality it can be said, that he:

1. knows his own capacities well enough to know which problems it is worth his while to try to solve;

2. is able to work out the most satisfactory way of solving these problems;

3. is prepared to accept tentative premises while recognising that they may later be discredited;

4. is able to act after due, but not excessive, collection of probable information.

What kind of teaching and learning leads towards such capabilities?

1. If self-standards and self-judgement are acquired as indicated in the last section, then an individual should have the necessary self-knowledge to estimate his own capabilities.

2. Granted the required learning sets and knowledge, whether an individual is skilled in recognising and solving appropriate problems will very possibly depend on the proficiency of his teachers in (*a*) freeing him individually, or in a group, to try out his own ideas, but (*b*) intervening to prevent frustration and rigidity and pointing the way to other more profitable procedures (cf. chapter 7, page 113).

3, 4. These capabilities depend upon recognition of the nature of human knowledge. Such recognition stems from learning sets, derived through a classroom relationship which allows, to learner and teacher alike, neither denial of error, nor pretence to certainty; and such recognition grows into intellectual honesty and humility.

'All human knowledge is uncertain, inexact and partial. To this doctrine we have not found any limitation whatever.' So Bertrand Russell concludes his famous essay on human knowledge (95).

LEARNING AND PERSONALITY

Little Albert's conditional fear, a boy's dislike of school and adult prejudice were instanced in chapter 4, as emotional attitudes acquired by classical conditioning. Chapter 7, page 107 stressed the importance of learning sets. Now it has been seen that, within the learner-teacher relationship, classical conditioning, learning sets and identification or imitation may lead to anxiety, co-operation and intellectual honesty, and these are but examples of the many *learned* emotive attitudes which pervade personality.

CONCLUSION

Learning is central to human development. The study of learning is essential for the study not only of cognitive development but also of the structure of personality. It is hoped that this book has prepared its readers for such studies.

SUMMARY

Teacher-learner relationships are crucial in relation to cognitive, social and achievement motivation, which in turn influence cognitive development and structure of personality.

FURTHER READING

Bruner (17) (18) and Holt (56) should prove enjoyable to all students who have been interested in this chapter. Berlyne is relevant to this chapter (9).

Bruner (19), a conference report, contains many interesting articles on the whole problem of learning.

Students interested in team teaching should read Lovell (68) (69).

Bibliography

1. Ackerman, W. I. & Levin, H. 'Effects of Training in Alternative Solution on Subsequent Problem Solving', *J. educ. Psychol.*, **49** (1958)
2. Apter, M. *The New Technology of Education* (Macmillan 1968)
3. Argyle, M. *Psychology and Social Problems* (Methuen 1964)
4. Aristotle, *de Memoria* II
5. Barnett, S. A. *A Study of Behaviour* (Methuen 1963)
6. Barnett, S. A. *Instinct and Intelligence* (MacGibbon & Kee 1967)
7. Bartlett, F. C. *Remembering* (Cambridge University Press 1932)
8. Bayliss, L. E. *Living Control Systems* (English Universities Press 1966)
9. Berlyne, D. E. *Conflict, Arousal and Curiosity* (McGraw Hill 1960)
10. Berlyne, D. E. 'Notes on Intrinsic Motivation and Intrinsic Reward in Relation to Instruction', in (19)
11. Bexton, W. H. *et al.* 'Effects of Decreased Variation in Sensory Environment', *Can. J. Psychol.*, **8** (1954)
12. Bibergall, J. A. 'Learning by Discovery', *Educ. Rev.* **18** (3) (1966)
13. Borger, R. & Seaborne, A. E. M. *The Psychology of Learning* (Pelican 1966)
14. Boycott, B. R. 'Learning in the Octopus', *Scientific American* (March 1965)
15. Broadhurst, P. L. *The Science of Animal Behaviour* (Pelican 1963)
16. Brown, J. S. *The Motivation of Behaviour* (McGraw-Hill 1961)
17. Bruner, J. S. *The Process of Education* (Vintage Books 1960)
18. Bruner, J. S. *Towards a Theory of Instruction* (Belknap Press 1966)
19. Bruner, J. S. (Ed.) *Learning about Learning*, Department of Health Education and Welfare (Washington 1966)
20. Bruning, J. L. 'Effects of Magnitude of Reward and Percentage of Reinforcement on a Lever-moving Response', *Child Dev.*, **35** (1964)
21. Butler, R. A. 'Discrimination Learning by Rhesus Monkeys to Visual Exploration Motivation', *J. comp. physiol. Psychol.*, **46** (1953)
22. Butler, R. A. 'The Effect of Deprivation of Visual Incentives on Visual Exploration Motivation in Monkeys', *Phys. Psych.*, **50**, 1957 (reported in (36))

23. Central Advisory Council for Education. *Children and their Primary Schools (Plowden Report)* (H M S O 1967)

24. Craft, M. *et al. Linking Home and School* (Longmans 1967)

25. Crandall, V. J. *et al.* 'Reinforcement Effects of Adult Reactions and Non-reactions on Children's Achievement Expectations', *Child Dev.*, **35** (1964)

26. Darlington, C. D. *Genetics and Man* (Pelican 1966)

27. De Cecco, J. P. (Ed.) *Human Learning in the School* (Holt, Rinehart & Winston 1963)

28. Deese, J. & Hulse, S. H. *The Psychology of Learning* (McGraw-Hill 1967)

29. Ebbinghaus, H. (trans. Ruger and Bussenius) *Memory* (Dover 1966)

30. Ellis, H. *The Transfer of Learning* (The Macmillan Company (N.Y.) 1965)

31. Evans, K. M. 'Teacher-Pupil Relationships', *Educ. Research,* **2** (1) (1959)

32. Eysenck, H. J. *Fact and Fiction in Psychology* (Pelican 1965)

33. Ferster, C. B. & Skinner, B. F. *Schedules of Reinforcement* (Appleton-Century-Crofts 1957)

34. Flugel, J. G. *A Hundred Years of Psychology* (Duckworth 1959)

35. Foss, B. M. (Ed.) *New Horizons in Psychology* (Pelican 1966)

36. Fowler, H. *Curiosity and Exploratory Behaviour* (The Macmillan Company (N.Y.) 1965)

37. Funkstein, D. *et al. Mastery of Stress* (Harvard Press 1957)

38. Galambos, R. & Sheatz, G. C. 'An Electro-encephalograph Study of Classical Conditioning', *Am. J. Physiol.*, **203** (1962)

39. Getzels, J. W. 'Creative Thinking, Problem-Solving and Instruction', in (54)

40. Gooch, S. & Kellmer-Pringle, M. L. *Four Years On* (Longmans 1966)

41. Goodall, J. van Lawick. Report of conversation in *Observer*, 30 April 1967

42. Gratch. G. 'An Exploratory Study of the Relation of Dependence upon Adult Approval and Age to Children's Risk-Taking', *Child Dev.*, **35** (1964)

43. Hamilton, Sir Wm. Quoted in (117)

44. Hargreaves, D. H. *Social Relations in a Secondary School* (Routledge & Kegan Paul 1967)

45. Harlow, H. F. 'The Formation of Learning Sets', in (30)

46. Harlow, H. F. & Kuenne, Margaret. 'Learning to Think', *Scientific American Offprint* 415 (August 1949)

47. Harlow, H. F. 'The Nature of Love', *Am. Psychol.*, **13** (1958)

48. Harlow, H. F. 'Love in Infant Monkeys', *Scientific American Offprint* 429 (June 1959)

49. Hays, P. *New Horizons in Psychiatry* (Pelican 1964)

50. Hebb, D. O. *Textbook of Psychology* (W. B. Saunders 1966)

51. Hendrickson, G. & Schroeder, W. 'Transfer of Training in Learning to Hit a Submerged Target', *J. educ. Psychol.*, **32** (1941)

52. Hilgard, E. R. *Introduction to Psychology* (Methuen 1958)

53. Hilgard, E. R. & Sears, P. S. 'The Teacher's Role in Motivation of the Learner', in (54)

54. Hilgard, E. R. (Ed.) *Theories of Learning and Instruction* (University of Chicago Press 1964)

55. Holland, A. L. & Matthews J. 'Application of Teaching Machine Concepts to Speech Pathology and Audiology', *ASHA*, **5** (1963)

56. Holt, J. *How Children Fail* (Dell Publishing Co 1964)

57. Hubel, D. H. & Wiesel, T. N. *J. Neurophysiol.*, **26** (1963)

58. Hudgins, B. B. *Problem Solving in the Classroom* (The Macmillan Company (N.Y.) 1966)

59. Hunter, I. M. L. *Memory* (Penguin 1964)

60. Hyden, H. 'Satellite Cells in the Nervous System', *Scientific American*, **205** (6) (1961)

61. Jacobson, A. L. 'Chemical Transfer of Learning', *Discovery*, **27** (2) (1966)

62. Jenkins, J. G. & Dallenbach, K. M. 'Oblivescence during Sleep and Waking', *Am. J. Psychol.*, **35** (1924)

63. Kagan, J. 'Motivational and Attitudinal Factors in Receptivity to Learning', in (19)

64. Lashley, K. S. 'In Search of the Engram', *Society of Experimental Biology Symposium No. 4* (Cambridge University Press 1950)

65. Lewis, D. J. 'Partial Reinforcement in a Gambling Situation', *J. exp. Psychol.*, **42** (1953)

66. *Life* Science Library. *The Cell* (1965)

67. *Life* Nature Library. *Evolution* (1964)

68. Lovell, K. 'Team Teaching', *Trends in Education*, **5** (Jan. 1967)

69. Lovell, K. *Team Teaching* (University of Leeds Institute of Education 1967)

70. Lovell, K. *An Introduction to Human Development* (Macmillan 1968)

71. Lowenstein, O. *The Senses* (Penguin 1966)

72. Manning, A. *An Introduction to Animal Behaviour* (Arnold 1967)

73. Medawar, P. B. *The Art of the Soluble* (Methuen 1967)

74. Melton, A. W. and Irwin, J. 'The Influence of Degree of Interpolated Learning on Retroactive Inhibition and the Overt Transfer of Specific Responses', *Am. J. Psychol.*, **53** (1940)

75. Miller, G. A. 'Information and Memory', *Scientific American Offprint* 419, (August 1956)

76. Miller, G. A. *Psychology: The Science of Mental Life* (Penguin 1966)

77. Miller, N. E. 'Fear as an Acquired Drive', *J. exp. Psychol.*, 38 (1948)

78. Milne, L. & M. *The Senses of Animals and Men* (Penguin 1965)

79. More, T. (trans. R. Robinson) *Utopia* (Walter Scott Publishing Co., no date)

80. Morgan, C. T. & King, R. A. *Introduction to Psychology* (McGraw-Hill 1966)

81. Morris, B. 'Mental Health in the Classroom', in *Studies in Education*, Number 7 (Evans 1955)

82. Mowrer, W. M. & O. H. 'Enuresis: A Method for its Study and Treatment', *Am. J. Orthopsychiat.*, 8 (1938)

83. Munn, N. L. 'Learning in Children', in *Manual of Child Psychology* (Ed. Carmichael, L.) (Wiley 1954)

84. Murray, E. J. *Motivation and Emotion* (Prentice-Hall 1964)

85. Nuffield Mathematics Project: 'I do and I understand' (Chambers & Murray 1967)

86. Olds, J. & Milner, P. 'Positive Reinforcement Produced by Electrical Stimulation of Septal Area and other Regions of Rat Brain', *J. comp. physiol. psychol.*, 47 (1954)

87. Olver, R. 'Tutor and Learner', in (19)

88. Pavlov, I. P. (trans. Anrep., G. V.) *Conditioned Reflexes* (Oxford University Press 1927)

89. Penfield, W. 'Functional Localisation in Temporal and Deep Sylvian Areas', in *The Brain and Human Behaviour* (Williams & Wilkins 1958)

90. Pribram, K. H. 'Neurological Notes on the Art of Education', in (54)

91. Polya, G. *How to Solve it* (Doubleday 1957)

92. Riesen, A. H. 'Arrested Vision', *Scientific American Offprint*, 408

93. Riess, B. F. 'Genetic Changes in Semantic Conditioning', *J. exp. Psychol.*, 36 (1946)

94. Riley, J. F. *Introducing Biology* (Penguin 1967)

95. Russell, B. A. W. *Human Knowledge: Its Scope and Limits* (Allen & Unwin 1948)

96. Sanford, F. H. *Psychology* (Wadsworth 1961)

97. Skinner, B. F. *Cumulative Record* (Methuen 1961)

98. Skinner, B. F. *Walden Two* (The Macmillan Company (N.Y.) 1948)

99. Sluckin, W. *Imprinting and Early Learning* (Methuen 1964)

100. Small, N. S. 'Notes on the Psychic Development of the Young White Rat', *Am. J. Psychol.*, 11 (1899)

101. Solomon, R. L. & Wynne, L. C. 'Traumatic Avoidance Learning Acquisition in Normal Dogs', *Psychol. Monograph,* **67,** No. 354 (1953)
102. Stenhouse, L. *Culture and Education* (Nelson 1967)
103. Stevenson, H. E. (Ed.) *Child Psychology* (University of Chicago Press 1963)
104. Thorndike, E. L. & Woodworth, R. S. 'The Influence of Improvement in One Mental Function upon the Efficiency of Other Functions', *Psychol. Rev.,* **8** (1901)
105. Thorpe, W. H. *Learning and Instinct in Animals* (Methuen 1963)
106. Tinbergen, N. *The Study of Instinct* (Clarendon Press 1951)
107. Torrance, E. P. *Guiding Creative Talent* (Prentice-Hall 1962)
108. Underwood, B. J. 'Forgetting', *Scientific American* (March 1964)
109. Underwood, B. J. 'Interference and Forgetting', *Psychol. Rev.,* **64** (1) (1957)
110. Vernon, J. *Inside the Black Room* (Penguin 1966)
111. Walter, W. G. *The Living Brain* (Penguin 1961)
112. Watson, J. B. *Behaviorism* (Kegan Paul 1931)
113. Williams, J. D. 'Teaching Problem-Solving', *Educ. Research,* **3** (1) (1960)
114. Wilmott, P. *Adolescent Boys of East London* (Routledge & Kegan Paul 1966)
115. Wittrock, M. C. & Twelker, P. A. 'Prompting and Feedback in the Learning, Retention and Transfer of Concepts', *Br. J. educ. Psychol.,* **34** (1) (1964)
116. Woodrow, H. 'The Effect of Type of Training upon Transference', *J. educ. Psychol.,* **18** (1927)
117. Woodworth, R. S. & Schlosberg, H. *Experimental Psychology* (Methuen 1954)
118. Young, J. Z. *The Memory System of the Brain* (Oxford University Press 1966)

Glossary

Note: Terms which are fully discussed in the text are not necessarily defined in the glossary.

AFFERENT NERVES. *See* Peripheral Nervous System.

ASSOCIATION. A general term referring to any connection formed through learning. S-R ASSOCIATION: a learned connection between a stimulus and a response. S-S ASSOCIATION: a learned connection between two stimuli.

ATTENTION. Focusing on certain aspects of current experience and neglecting others. Interests, motives and perceptual set or expectancy influence what is selected for attention.

ATTITUDE. A readiness to respond in a particular manner to some circumstance or idea.

AUTONOMIC NERVOUS SYSTEM. A division of the nervous system serving glands and smooth (involuntary) muscles. One of its functions is to control internal changes in the body during emotion. It is divided into the *sympathetic system* (most active in aroused states) and the *parasympathetic system* (most active in quiescent states).

CENTRAL NERVOUS SYSTEM. The brain and spinal cord.

CEREBRAL CORTEX. The grey matter which covers the largest part of the brain, the cerebrum.

CHROMOSOMES. Stainable threads in the nucleus of cells. When stained, the threads are observable under the microscope. Chromosomes carry the GENES.

COGNITIVE DEVELOPMENT. The process by which human beings increase their power to acquire and use knowledge.

CONCEPT. A learned tendency to use and respond to signs which indicate some property or relationship common to a series of STIMULUS OBJECTS OR EVENTS.

DNA Deoxyribonucleic acid. The information-carrying material of which a GENE is composed.

DRIVE. Impetus to action. General drive leads to exploration and activity. Specific drives satisfy specific needs by reducing tension.

EFFERENT NERVES. *See* Peripheral Nervous System.

EFFECTORS. Organs of response (muscles and glands.)

ELECTROENCEPHALOGRAM (EEG). A record of electrical fluctuations (changing potential) in the brain ('brain waves') usually obtained by placing electrodes on the skull.

ETHOLOGIST. A zoologist or naturalist who studies animal behaviour, especially instinctive behaviour and its relation to learned behaviour.

FEEDBACK. In relation to learning, the term means returned information concerning the results of an act.

GENE. A unit of DNA with a fixed location in a CHROMOSOME. Genes are responsible for transmission and development of particular inherited characteristics.

HABIT. A learned sequence of behaviour readily repeated in response to certain stimulus conditions.

HABITUATION. Decline in frequency of performance of an act as a result of continued repetition of the stimulus which formerly prompted the act.

HOMEOSTASIS. The maintenance of constancy in the internal environment of an organism. According to homeostatic theories of MOTIVATION, organisms are driven to bring about this state.

IDENTIFICATION. The tendency of children and young people to acquire ATTITUDES And HABITS by copying, in part unconsciously, the behaviour of admired adults.

IMAGERY. Revived sensory experience occurring in the absence of stimulation of a sense organ.

IMITATION. Copying the behaviour of another.

IMPRINTING. Learning, during an early sensitive period, to follow or approach an object, in normal circumstances a member of the same species, usually the mother.

INCENTIVE. An object or circumstance which prompts or rewards behaviour.

MOTIVATION. State which determines the selective and organised way in which an individual will act.

NUCLEUS. Body containing the chromosomes, present in nearly all cells of plants and animals.

PERIPHERAL NERVOUS SYSTEM. The system of nerves outside the CENTRAL NERVOUS SYSTEM. Afferent nerves carry impulses from sense organs to the central nervous system. Efferent (motor) nerves carry impulses from the CENTRAL NERVOUS SYSTEM to EFFECTORS.

PRIMATES. The order of mammals which contains monkeys, apes and men.

PROTOZOA. Group of animals (usually microscopic) which consist of only one cell and at least one well-defined nucleus.

RECEPTOR. Sometimes defined as sense organ and sometimes as nerve endings in sense organs.

REFLEX. A rapid, consistent, unlearned and usually involuntary response to a stimulus.

SERVOMECHANISM. A self-regulating system. At any time the difference between the present and the required state of the system is automatically fed back to it. This information activates the system until the difference is eliminated.

STIMULUS OBJECT OR EVENT. Provides energy which excites organisms. In creatures with nervous systems, the energy is transformed into neural energy.

SUBJECTS. Individuals taking part in experiments as members of control or experimental groups.

Index